Hiking the AT in the Virginias

U.S. Geological Survey benchmarks, like the one flanked by the author's battered boots, officially pinpoint the path of the Appalachian Trail (AT).

Hiking the AT in the Virginias

A Septuagenarian's Journey

Photographs and stories
by Dave Pruett

with a foreword
by Mills Kelly

George F. Thompson Publishing
in association with the
Center for the Study of Place

Day-hiker Suzanne Fiederlein, the author's wife,
enjoying the Henry Lanum Loop Trail.

To Suzanne and Elena
and to trail angels everywhere

Great views of historic Harpers Ferry and the Shenandoah River from Maryland Heights are accessible from the AT by steep blue- and red-blazed trails. The overlook draws droves of day-hikers: young and old, fit and hoping to become fit, American and international. The Shenandoah flows into the Potomac River at this historic confluence. (Also, see page 76.)

Note: All photographs are by the author, except as noted in a caption.

CONTENTS

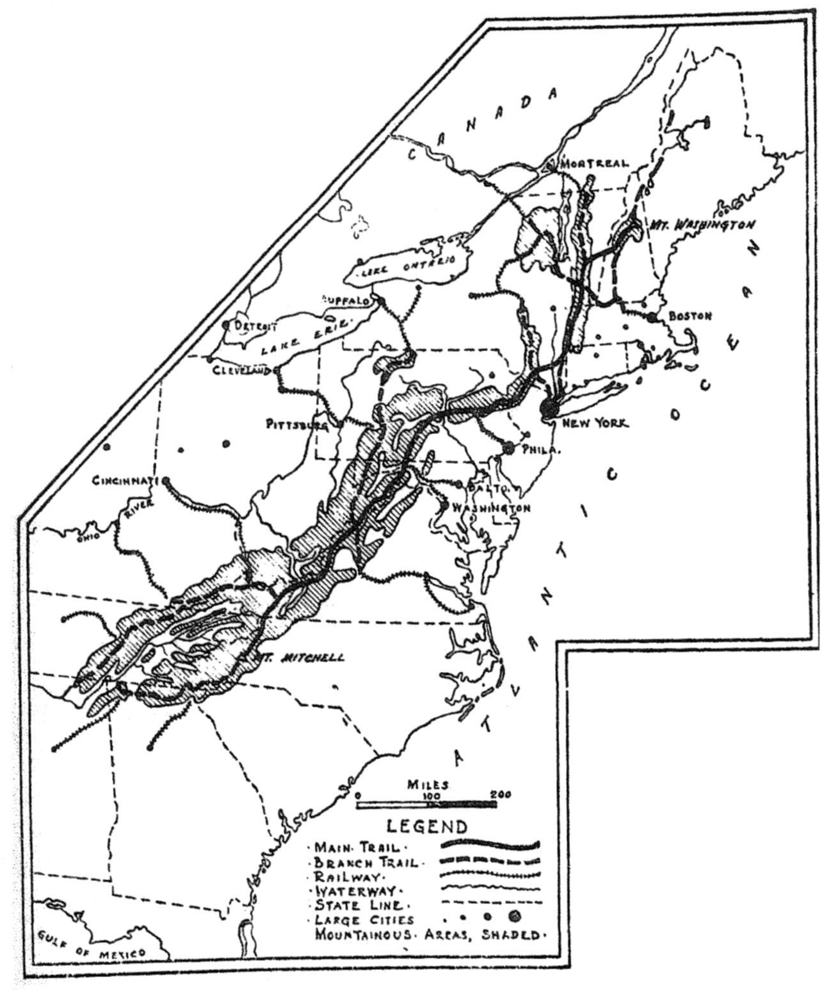

Benton MacKaye's original map of the Appalachian Trail appeared in "The Appalachian Trail: A Project in Regional Planning," in *The Journal of the American Institute of Architects*, Vol. 9 (October 1921). The article and map were reprinted later that year in a brochure titled "A Project for an Appalachian Trail," produced by the AIA's Committee on Community Planning, with an introduction by Clarence S. Stein, the committee's chairman. MacKaye's map depicted a main trail from Mount Washington in New Hampshire to Mount Mitchell in North Carolina as well as various existing or proposed branch trails.The map's caption read, "Area shown contains more than half the population of the United States and over one third the population of Canada." (Also, see page 12.)

FOREWORD

100 Years and Counting

Mills Kelly

JUST BEFORE HIS DEATH IN 1975, Benton MacKaye, the man who dreamed up the Appalachian Trail in 1921, gave a final interview to a long-time friend from his days working with the U.S. Forest Service. MacKaye was ninety-six years old but still kept a close eye on the trail that was his most successful idea. During their chat, the interviewer informed MacKaye that there were at least 200 hikers out on the AT that year attempting what we now call a "thru-hike," hoping to complete the entire trail in one year. MacKaye was not impressed.

Instead of marveling at the remarkable feat of covering nearly 2,200 miles of mountain trail in one hiking season, MacKaye said, "I want to give a prize to the one who took the longest to hike the trail."[1] He went on to explain that, in his view, "thru-hikers" were in much too much of a hurry to get from one end of the trail to the other and that hurrying like that got in the way of actually *seeing* the mountains, the plants, the animals, and the vistas. Only when hikers slowed down would they actually have the opportunity to really see.

Most of what we know about hiking on America's most iconic long-distance hiking trail comes to us from accounts by those who have attempted a thru-hike, whether they made it from one end to the other or not, and those accounts are all of a type. They followed the classic hero quest narrative—I came, I strove against daunting odds to achieve my goal, I succeeded (or failed), and along the way I learned something important about myself or my life changed in some fundamental way. As inspiring as these thru-hiker accounts can be, too often they tell us a lot about the hiker and not very much about the trail itself and the many ecosystems the AT passes through.

Set in contrast to those hero quests, Dave Pruett's "section-hike" of the Appalachian Trail in the Virginias is exactly what Benton MacKaye had in mind. Pruett hiked slowly, he paused constantly to observe the natural world around him, to chat with other hikers and residents of towns along the trail, and, most importantly, he *saw* the places he passed through. Perhaps the single biggest lesson from all that seeing is that, as Pruett points out early on in this delightful book, "There isn't just one AT. Each hiker experiences a unique one."

Each year between three and four million people set foot on the Appalachian Trail, and of those only a tiny, tiny fraction attempt a thru-hike. The rest are there for a few hours, a few days, or perhaps a few weeks, and, like Pruett, the version of the AT they experience is ephemeral. Views change with the seasons, friendships with other hikers begin and end quickly, hardships are overcome and soon forgotten, a bear walks across the trail just ahead of you and then is gone in a rush, a storm rumbles just to the north of you but never quite makes it to your ridgetop, stars wheel across the sky above your tent in a dance too old to comprehend, and other hikers pass by with a wave or a nod.

Dave Pruett captures all this impermanence as he leads the reader from Harpers Ferry, West Virginia, at the confluence of the Shenandoah and Potomac Rivers, to Damascus on the Virginia-Tennessee line. The further one dives into his stories of places, people, nature, and his own ruminations as he walked, the more insight one gains into just how different it is to hike the AT at a slow pace. For one thing, hikers like Pruett who are on the trail to *see* have so many more options for enjoyment of the Appalachian Mountains. Throughout the book, Pruett treats the reader to descriptions of what one might find by following one of the hundreds of blue-blazed "spur trails" that connect with the AT. Half a mile here takes you to Crabtree Falls, half a mile there leads to the summit of Mount Rogers, the highest point in Virginia. Thru-hikers rarely take these spur trails because they are in a hurry, but when the goal of one's hike is to experience the Appalachian Trail as a pathway through the many and varied ecosystems of the Appalachians in Virginia and West Virginia, taking one of the many spur trails Pruett describes merely adds to the overall hiking experience.

The AT is not only a forest trail. In southwestern Virginia it traverses "balds" that recall the Highlands of Scotland, it passes through many pastures and meadows, crisscrosses the Blue Ridge Parkway and Skyline Drive, and takes advantage of many highway bridges and several purpose-built hiker bridges.* The variety of the landscapes in the Virginias described in this book make it abundantly clear just how different the trail is from one day to the next and how staggeringly beautiful those landscapes can be. I have hiked most of the sections of the AT in the two Virginias and I couldn't agree more with Pruett that "both forest and meadow feed the soul."

By joining Dave Pruett on his journey through the Virginias, his words and his many wonderful photographs will give you the opportunity to feed your soul vicariously. But I hope this book will encourage you to really see the Appalachian Mountains for yourself. And, if it does, I also hope you'll slow down and really notice what you are seeing.

* Note: Terms such as "thru-hiker," "section-hiker," "spur trail," and "balds" are defined in the *Glossary* (pages 189–90).

Many hikers bring along binoculars not only for birdwatching, but also to focus in on enchanting bird's-eye-views such as this from Maryland Heights of the Shenandoah River and historic Harpers Ferry, West Virginia (see page 6). Even as the actual half-way point of the current 2,197.4-mile-long AT (3,536 kilometers) is in Pine Grove Furnace State Park near Gardners, Pennsylvania, Harpers Ferry (AT mile marker 1,023.1) has long been the AT's psychological midpoint.* The Appalachian Trail Conservancy (ATC) has its headquarters and visitor center here. (Also, see pages 21 and 79.)

* Note: Conversions to metric units are provided for the the benefit of international readers, visitors, and AT hikers in all the captions and notes as well as in the *Introduction* and *Acknowledgments*. Beginning with *Chapter One: Trails*, conversions to metric units in the text are self-evident or easily found online and on smartphones.

Benton MacKaye revised his original 1921 map of the AT (see page 8) and prepared this version for presentation at the first meeting of the Appalachian Trail Conference, held in the Raleigh Hotel in Washington, D.C., on March 2, 1925. Besides depicting the main proposed trail and possible branch trails, MacKaye also located five "pivotal sections," on which he urged trail builders to concentrate their efforts.

Hiking the AT in the Virginias

The author stands at the celebratory milestone of 700 miles (1,127 kilometers) north of the AT's southern terminus (atop Singer Mountain near Forest Service Road 42 near Ellijay, Georgia) or, equivalently, one-third of the full distance for a NOBO (northbound) thru-hiker.* The marker is located at the exact GPS point corresponding to mile 700 on the FarOut (formerly GutHook) trail app.

* Note: As mentioned on page 10, terms such as "NOBO" and "thru-hiker" appear in the *Glossary* (pages 189–90).

INTRODUCTION

Hiking the AT

**Every act a ceremony.
Every word a prayer.
Every walk a pilgrimage.
Every place a shrine.[1]**
—CHARLES EISENSTEIN

HIKING THE APPALACHIAN TRAIL is both ordeal and pilgrimage. Its vistas, meadows, forest floors, shelters, and watering holes are at once mere way stations and holy shrines. It's all a matter of perspective.

Conceived by Benton MacKaye in 1921 and completed in 1937, the Appalachian Trail, affectionately known as the "AT," is one of the longest footpaths (hiking-only trails) on Earth, traversing the spine of North America's ancient Appalachian Mountains. From its origin on Springer Mountain, Georgia, to its terminus on Mount Katahdin, Maine, the AT winds 2,197.4 miles (3,536 kilometers).[2] Along the way, it passes through twelve additional states: North Carolina, Tennessee, Virginia, West Virginia, Maryland, Pennsylvania, New Jersey, New York, Connecticut, Massachusetts, Vermont, and New Hampshire.

The states of Virginia and West Virginia contain the most and the least miles on the AT: 531.7 miles (855.7 kilometers) in VA and 2.4 miles (3.9 kilometers) in WV, while jointly sharing another 25.3 miles (40.7 kilometers) along their common border just south of Harpers Ferry and further south on the ridgeline of Peters Mountain.[3] Although I grew up in West Virginia, I have lived in Virginia for most of my life. Both states have more than their fair share of natural beauty. For the purposes of this book, the two Virginias are considered together, altogether fitting since they were once conjoined before the Civil War cleaved West Virginia from Virginia in 1862.

For most of my life I've lived within an hour's drive of the AT, and, for much of that time, I have dreamt sporadically of hiking its entirety. Although in my twenties and thirties I completed a number of section-hikes with my brother or a buddy, completing the AT has remained just a dream. Then, at the age of forty, beset by an unexpected urge to solo trek, I strapped on a JanSport backpack large enough for a bathtub, filled it with fifty-four pounds (24.5 kilograms) of gear and sustenance, and hiked north on the AT out of Damascus, Virginia, bound for the high country of Mount Rogers and Grayson Highlands State Park. After a schlep of nine miles (14.5 kilometers), mostly uphill, I collapsed and camped right beside the trail, too exhausted to search for a better spot. Each day thereafter I grew stronger. By day four, lugging a pack for fifteen miles (24.1 kilometers) seemed the most natural thing in the world and taking it off at the end of the day occasioned the euphoria of feeling weightless. Dad, who'd just retired, picked me up in the afternoon of the fifth day, and we spent a sweet night with Grandma at the family cabin, my halfway house back to civilization. I'd knocked off fifty-five miles (88.5 kilometers) in all and had a glorious adventure in the process.

Career and family intervened, and few such opportunities presented themselves again until I semi-retired at sixty-four. Hiking the full AT and peddling across country remained on the bucket list, but was I over the hill? Most likely. Certainly my JanSport days were over. The external-frame beast and its archaic gear gave way to an internal-frame North Face, a lightweight down sleeping bag, and a three-pound MSR tent. Much as I loved that faithful brass Svea white-gas stove, it went to pasture, replaced by a 1.7-ounce (fifty-milliliter) titanium contraption atop a five-ounce (148-milliliter) propane canister.

In September 2013, my second summer into retirement, my wife, Suzanne, dropped me late one morning in Harpers Ferry, West Virginia, the rough midpoint of the entire AT, and I naively headed south and uphill from the Shenandoah River with forty pounds (eighteen kilograms) of gear, including seven days of food. I'd hoped to make 100 miles (160 kilometers) in a week and to convince myself that the twenty-four intervening years since that first solo trek had not robbed me of much stamina. Oh, was I wrong.

At midday on day three, I showered at Bears Den Hiker Hostel and Trail Center, a mecca for "thru-hikers." There, thirty bucks gets you a bed, shower, washer, pizza, and pint of Ben and Jerry's. I left immediately after the shower, cognizant that, should I remain longer, I'd succumb to the Sirens of Comfort. From Bears Den the AT snakes over the infamous boulder-strewn "Roller Coaster" that fatigues even veteran Appalachian Trailers, and from there to the threshold of graceful Sky Meadows State Park at U.S. 50 near Paris, Virginia.

On the morning of day five, not far from Sky Meadows, with thirty-four miles (54.7 kilometers) under my belt and a painful blister at the end of a toe, I awakened to terrifying numbness along my right arm. Fearing a heart attack, I popped a baby aspirin—always a companion—and called Suzanne to rescue me. With no other symptoms of heart trouble, I calmed down and began to explore other reasons for the worrisome numbness.

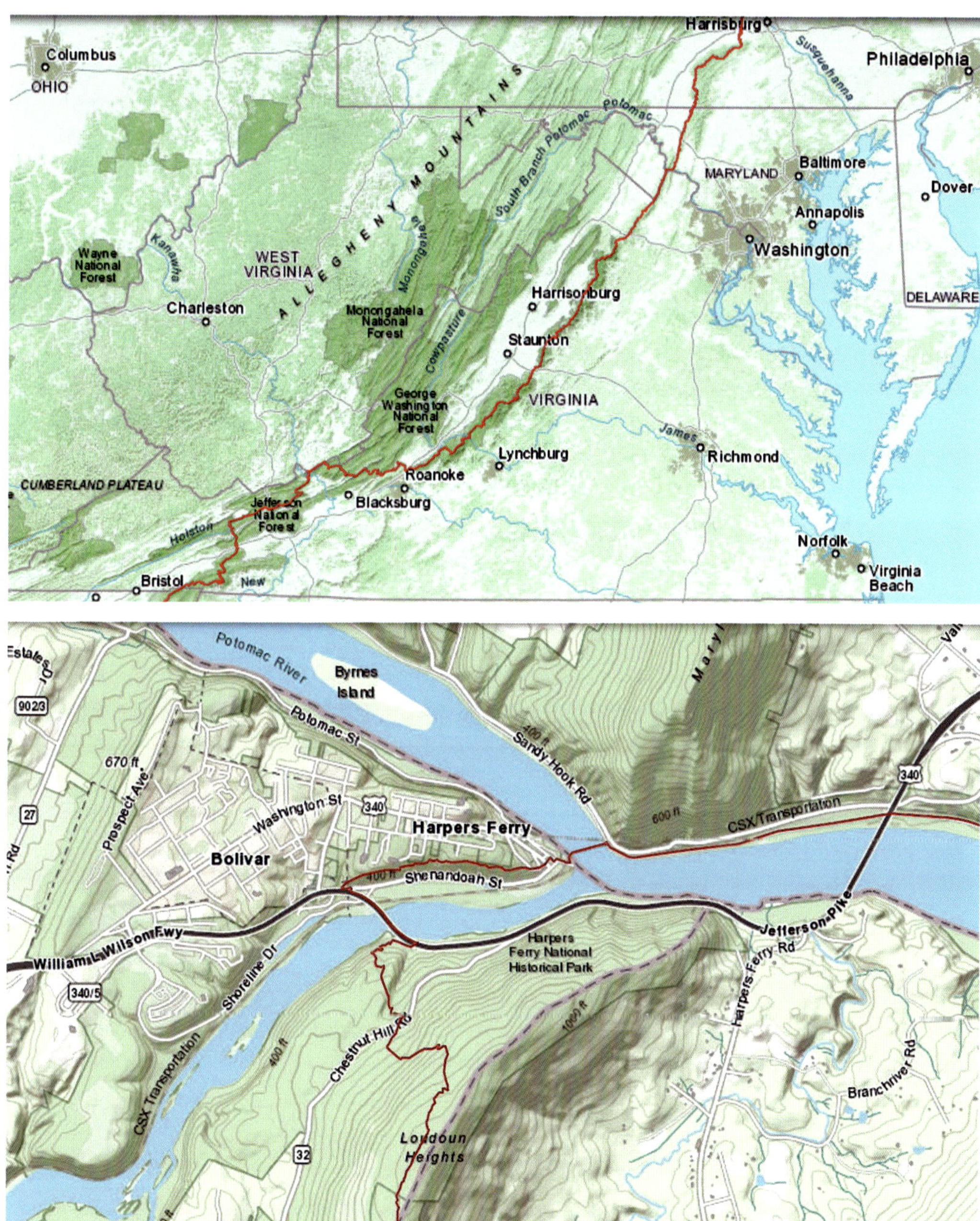

TOP: The AT traverses the spine of the Blue Ridge Mountains of the Virginias, as shown in red on this regional map extracted from the Appalachian Trail Conservancy's (ATC's) interactive online map. BOTTOM: A northbound (NOBO) AT hiker leaves Virginia by crossing the iconic Shenandoah River into West Virginia and then shortly exits West Virginia by crossing the Potomac River into Maryland. The Shenandoah joins the Potomac at Harpers Ferry, where Virginia, West Virginia, and Maryland meet, as seen on the ATC's interactive online map.

In the time it took Suzanne to arrive from Harrisonburg, an alternative theory about my symptoms surfaced. Years ago I'd damaged an elbow from daily lugging a leaden briefcase to and from work. While navigating the "Roller Coaster," I'd relied heavily for balance on a hiking pole in my right hand, the stronger one. The constant pressure along my arm had revived the old elbow injury and pinched a nerve. It wasn't a heart attack, but it was time to throw in the towel. Three weeks elapsed before full feeling returned in the arm.

The next summer, with expectations trimmed, I tried again, anticipating a three-day inaugural trek. Two buddies dropped me at U.S. 522 south of Front Royal and joined me for a few miles as I hiked up into Shenandoah National Park, headed south. Eight miles (12.9 kilometers) and 2,000 feet (610 meters) in elevation later, now alone, I set up camp on a rocky side trail, moments ahead of a thunderstorm. Then on the second day, while pounding downhill toward a campground with the promise of a shower, I blew out my left knee. Worse, there was no shower, only a "comfort station."

This time the injury was severe: I'd mangled the meniscus. Another rescue. For two months I limped in pain, then spent two more months recovering from arthroscopic surgery. It seemed my backpacking days had ended abruptly. An orthopedist said: "No more backpacking—try biking instead."

No doubt good advice from a physical point of view, it was suspect from a psychological one. Fortunately, my general practitioner recognized the dilemma and gave tentative blessings to continued trekking, with provisos. During the spring of recovery following surgery, I pondered options and sought a compromise with myself. A reasonable accommodation emerged: Were I to limit the number of days per trek to three, the maximum pack weight to thirty pounds (13.6 kilograms), and the maximum distance to eight miles (thirteen kilometers) per day, might I keep trekking long enough to complete all of the AT in the Virginias, a full quarter of the trail's entirety? If so, in the bargain, with daily distance expectations trimmed, might there be more occasions to stop and smell the wildflowers along the way?

The plan worked. The third summer, I completed five short section-hikes, each about twenty miles (thirty-two kilometers) long, finishing the trail through nearby Shenandoah National Park. By the end of each section, the troublesome knee was sore and stiff. But each time it recovered after a few days of rest and acupuncturist-recommended exercises to open the joint. A little prophylactic ibuprofen before hiking also helped tamp down swelling. And, sure enough, a turtle's pace had distinct advantages: The experience became richer.

By the end of the fourth summer, having turned sixty-eight, I'd completed all sections of the AT between the Potomac and James Rivers. Most memorable was the high country near Cole Mountain, where the trail wound through open meadows. Even in thick rain and fog, I found the meadows delightful, a stark contrast to the cloistered woods.

Seven more summers have since elapsed without serious incident (although I did spill off the trail once when a hiking pole cut through the berm on the downhill edge of the trail, my support vanishing in an instant). I've crossed the James River on the Memorial Foot Bridge and managed the long slog up to Thunder Ridge on the Blue Ridge Parkway near Peaks of Otter. I've done Virginia's Triple Crown: Tinker Cliffs, Dragons Tooth, and McAfee Knob, all in a twenty-mile (thirty-two kilometer) stretch near Roanoke.[4] I've conquered Mountain Lake Wilderness and Peters, Pearis, Brushy, Little Walker, Big Walker, Glade, Garden, The Priest, and many other unnamed mountains. I've hiked for miles in tunnels of rhododendron along Dismal Creek (twenty-five miles or forty kilometers from where I grew up), seen my first-ever scarlet tanager on Brushy Mountain, splurged for a night at the beguiling Woods Hole Hostel on Pearis Mountain, and reveled in the high country of Grayson Highlands State Park. I've met fellow hikers from many walks and stations of life and from different countries. I've survived thunderstorms, been lulled to sleep by choruses of crickets and tree frogs, and awakened to symphonies of bird song. Oh, and I've narrowly avoided a murderer.[5]

In August 2019, I completed my last major section-hike in Virginia, Garden Mountain, the subject of the Epilogue. In 2020 and 2021, I took two small victory laps by section-hiking Maryland's forty-one miles (sixty-six kilometers) of AT. And in 2023, at age seventy-five, I filled in two short gaps in Virginia, totaling ten miles (sixteen kilometers), that I'd initially missed due to circumstances. It's been quite the adventure, full of indelible images.

In truth, there isn't just one AT. Each hiker experiences a unique one. With the gradual flux of season and the rapid one of weather, a given section of trail can offer completely different moods at different times of year, or different times of day. There are times when the trail experience is so physically punishing that I doubt my sanity for pushing on. But on the flip side of a shower, beer, and good night's sleep in a soft bed, I'm eager to experience more of the AT's moods and challenges.

A few years ago, I met a thru-hiker who had completed America's hiking triple crown: the Pacific Crest National Scenic Trail, the Pacific Northwest Trail, and the Appalachian Trail. I inquired as to his favorite. Without hesitation he replied: "The AT," which he was hiking a second time. Why? The variety encountered along the AT—in vegetation, terrain, weather, vistas, and rock formations—can seem infinite, even when trekking only in the Virginias. One never tires of the sensual smorgasbord.

When I began hiking the trail, I relied on maps and carried a compass, the latter never used. Maps have since given way to apps. In 2016, I purchased a small iPhone. A number of reasons vie for this Luddite's entry into the twenty-first century, the principle one being that a phone doubles as a lightweight camera. Most of the photos that appear herein were shot with an iPhone SE. I didn't have it the entire eleven seasons of this journey, so some of my favorite spots on the trail have been revisited on day-hikes, with a Nikon. And although the lion's share of the photos in this volume are my own, friends and family contributed several shots that I missed and for which I am most grateful.

Unlike most of the younger crowd, I don't listen to music or podcasts while hiking, but I do find these helpful in biding time in a tent or soothing the drift-off into sleep. For several years, I've relied on Guthook (now FarOut), an app that uses GPS to pinpoint one's location on the trail and lists all trail features relevant to hikers: water sources, shelters, hostels, overlooks, campsites, showers, restaurants, nearby towns, and more. An extraordinary resource, it even tracks hikers' helpful comments. Finally, when solo trekking, having an SOS feature on a phone is a comfort.

Hiking the AT is, at any age, not to be undertaken lightly. Best to familiarize oneself with its rigors well in advance and plan accordingly. For a well-rounded introduction to the AT, read David Emblidge's anthology: *The Appalachian Trail Reader* (Oxford, 1996). Here, one will find the inspiration for and history of the trail as well as experiences of those who have hiked it in part or in its entirety. As the jacket copy states, "A patchwork quilt of voices, both eloquent and raw, *The Appalachian Trail Reader* presents a rich introduction . . . for those planning a walking trip, and a vivid scrapbook for those who have already hiked its mountains and valley."[6] And, for a helpful introduction to how the idea of the AT came to be, turn to Larry Anderson's indispensable biography: *Benton MacKaye: Conservationist, Planner, and Creator of the Appalachian Trail* (2002).

The product of the determination of visionaries, the sweat equity of hundreds of volunteers, and a model public-private partnership, the AT is a national treasure cherished at home and abroad. That partnership involves the National Park Service, Appalachian Trail Conservancy (ATC), thirty-one volunteer clubs, and several dozen land-management agencies, even as overall administrative responsibility for the AT's 250,000 acres (101,171 hectares) of corridor lands falls to the National Park Service.[7] On average, the corridor spans but 1,000 feet (305 meters) in width, making the AT, in one sense, a long and skinny national greenway. Most of the corridor is owned outright. Occasionally, utilities or land owners grant narrow rights-of-way through private property.

Preservation and management of the AT, however, is the work of the ATC, a nonprofit organization established in 1925 and headquartered in Harpers Ferry, West Virginia. Affiliated with the ATC are dozens of regional clubs whose volunteers undertake the nitty-gritty maintenance and repair. They also work closely with land-management agencies to preserve surrounding high-priority landscapes. Among the largest of the clubs is the Potomac Appalachian Trail Club (PATC), which has a volunteer workforce of more than 600, maintains sixty shelters and cabins, and keeps in good repair more than 1,000 miles (1,609 kilometers) of trail, including 240 miles (386 kilometers) of the AT in Virginia, West Virginia, Maryland, and Pennsylvania.[8] In the final tallying, the AT is nothing short of miraculous. In recognition of its uniqueness, the National Trails Act of 1968 designated the AT a national scenic trail worthy of federal protection.

TOP: A main attraction at the ATC's Visitor Center is a relief map of the AT in its entirety, from Georgia to Maine, pondered long by hikers both wistful and accomplished.
BOTTOM: The entrance to the ATC's Visitor Center, where hikers find maps, hats, bandanas, socks, T-shirts, water bottles, other memorabilia, as well as good advice and kindred spirits. The ATC's headquarters is in the same building on the left (see page 79).

Despite that designation and the tender-loving-care of hundreds of volunteers and professionals, the AT, like many public treasures, faces mounting threats. These include over use, sometimes inadequate funding for maintenance, invasive species, encroachment from private interests, and climate change. But the most immediate threats have come from two massive natural-gas pipelines in planning and construction since 2014: the Mountain Valley Pipeline (MVP), which crosses the AT on Peters Mountain, and the Atlantic Coast Pipeline (ACP), which was slated to tunnel under the AT and Blue Ridge Parkway at Reeds Gap.

From the beginning, opposition to the pipelines—from an unlikely alliance of Tea Partiers, farmers opposed to eminent domain, and environmental advocates—was fierce and unrelenting, for good reasons. First, the construction itself is environmentally devastating. Second, each completed pipeline would cross hundreds of streams and tributaries, and construction runoff would degrade water quality for communities, towns, and cities downstream. Third, such pipelines, at forty-two inches (107 centimeters) in diameter and carrying 100 atmospheres pressure, are inherently dangerous, particularly because their routes traverse unstable karst terrain. Fourth, there's no pressing public need for this infrastructure; it's for private gain. And, lastly, such projects lock in decades of reliance on fossil fuels at the very moment when climate considerations demand a national and international weaning off of fossil energy. Proponents tout jobs and the ongoing necessity of energy as benefits, but the facts reveal that any new jobs will be short-lived, the environmental devastation and hazard long-lived, and energy shareholders the only major beneficiaries.

In the case of the ACP, the opposition against energy giants Dominion Energy Virginia and Duke Energy has been likened to a David and Goliath struggle, and in the beginning no one aligned with David expected to win. In retrospect, though, a Gulliver and Lilliputians analogy is more apt. Turns out there are a lot of Lilliputians. A partial list of the opposition-alliance partners includes national organizations such as the ATC, the Natural Resources Defense Council, the Sierra Club, and the Southern Environmental Law Center, in addition to a host of local organizations, among them Appalachian Voices, Alliance for the Shenandoah Valley, Friends of Nelson County, Virginia Interfaith Power and Light, Virginia Organizing, Climate Action Alliance of the Valley, and Wild Virginia.

A defining moment of resistance to the ACP pipeline occurred on February 19, 2019, when Poor People's Campaign organizer Rev. William Barbour and former Vice-President Al Gore teamed up to host an electrifying town-hall meeting in Union Hill, Virginia, proposed site of a compressor station. The meeting linked issues of racial and environmental justice, Union Hill being an historical African-American community whose culture and health would have been compromised by the construction and operation of the plant.

On a beautiful fall day in 2018, citizens from all walks of life and political persuasions gathered to oppose the 600-mile-long (966 kilometers) Atlantic Coast Pipeline (ACP), which, had it been completed, would have crossed the AT at Reeds Gap, site of the protest. In July 2020, developers of the ACP canceled the project, in large part due to economic and environmental realities and well-organized, informed, and relentless bi-partisan opposition.

Following six years of conflict, with passions high on both sides, the impossible happened. On July 5, 2020, *The Richmond Times-Dispatch* dropped this bombshell: "The Atlantic Coast Pipeline is dead, abandoned by Dominion Energy and its partner, Duke Energy, after the $8 billion project reached a regulatory dead end."[9]

The environmental victory over the ACP was the result of "death by a thousand cuts," a strategy articulated in 2014 by Nancy Sorrells, well-known local historian, opposition ringleader, founder of the pipeline resistance group Augusta County Alliance, and a force of nature. Opposition took every imaginable form: from letter-writing campaigns and protests to influence regulatory agencies and public opinion, law suits to challenge lax permitting processes by federal and state agencies, guest-speaking at local churches to get the word out, tree-sitting along pipeline rights-of-way, petitions to Dominion Energy shareholders, and even a citizen's air force to monitor construction violations from on high.[10]

Such fierce battles are costly to both sides. The 303-mile (488-kilometer) MVP weathered its opposition to enter service on June 14, 2024. It survived despite the heroic efforts of "Red" Terry and others like her. In April 2018, at sixty-one years of age, "Red" climbed thirty feet (nine meters) to a platform suspended between two trees on Bent Mountain and camped there for weeks to protest eminent domain for the pipeline's right-of-way through her ancestral property. She eventually lost the battle when a judge ruled "Red" and her daughter in contempt, and local authorities prepared to charge her with trespassing on her own property. Still, #StandWithRed went viral, and "Red" became a local folk hero.

The greatest long-term threat to the AT and the surrounding national parks and forests is the challenge that haunts us all: climate instability. Because climatic changes are slow and subtle, data and valid science are necessary to tease out fact from ideological noise and to assess the seriousness of the threats. To these ends, in 2005 New England's Appalachian Mountain Club (AMC), which predates the ATC, launched Mountain Watch, a citizen-scientist program in *phenology*: the study and recording of the cyclic seasonal changes of plant and animal life in relation to climate.[11] For example, are the seasonal patterns of flowering plants static or shifting over time? And what better source of field scientists than the hordes of AT hikers? In 2013, the AMC expanded the Mountain Watch program into the "A.T. Seasons" program by combining phenological data with weather data from the Mount Washington Observatory in New Hampshire. The A.T. Seasons program is also affiliated with the National Phenology Network, which takes advantage of crowd-sourced data. Already, these programs are revealing trends: spring leaf-outs along the AT corridor are occurring three to four weeks earlier in recent decades, treelines are moving higher up mountainsides, and invasive species are spreading. Such data are essential to stewards of the AT by pinpointing, for example, when to remove invasive plants during a season with the least likelihood of their return and when invasive insects like the emerald ash borer (*Agrilus planipennis*) are most vulnerable. And, of course, the historic torrential rains and subsequent floods of July 2023, especially in Vermont, Pennsylvania, and upstate New York, remind us of how powerful storms can develop suddenly and violently, causing human deaths and catastrophic damage.

Whereas these climate-related changes might not seem particularly worrying, they hint of increased hazards both for the forests and those who wander them. The sad reality is that there's evidence that the devastation of the majestic eastern hemlock (*Tsuga canadensis*) by an invasive insect, the Hemlock woolly adelgid (*Adelges tsugae*), has been exacerbated by a warming climate. And the Environmental Protection Agency also links to warming trends a doubling of the incidence of Lyme disease since 1991. Lyme disease may be the greatest hazard faced by AT hikers. It takes constant vigilance to keep the AT, its environs, and its wayfarers healthy. Sometimes it's an uphill struggle.

But back to the good news: The attentive hiker will never be bored on the AT. Every mile affords ample opportunities for surprise or awe. Tunnels and thickets of rhododendron and mountain laurel, ever-changing rock formations, unencumbered vistas, rippling streams and brooks, nighttime chirps, musty smells, blazing wildflowers, walking in mist

Common sights on Virginia's AT: lichen-covered rocks and flowering mountain laurel (*Kalmia latifolia*), whose blooms grace the trail as early as mid-to-late-April but more often in May and June.

and clouds, and immense solitude . . . These and other moments on the Appalachian Trail beckon my soul when reason and comfort say, "No, stay home."

Here, then, is a septuagenarian's journey and my attempt to capture quicksilver: the beauty, moods, and magic of the AT in the Virginias that I call home. As Benton MacKaye wrote: "The ultimate purpose [of the AT]? There are three things: (1) to walk; (2) to see; (3) to see what you see."[12]

Sturdy signposts, ubiquitous at Appalachian Trail (AT) crossings, alert hikers of distances and side trails. At this location, the Loft Mountain Campground store awaits nearby with the promise of showers, sustenance, and good company.

ONE

Trails

These mountains, in several ways rivaling the western scenery, are within a day's ride from centers containing more than half of the population of the United States.[1]

—BENTON MACKAYE

WALKING THE AT OF THE VIRGINIAS RANGES from a stroll in the park—quite literally at Harpers Ferry National Historic Park, Shenandoah National Park, and Sky Meadows and Grayson Highlands State Parks—to a grueling slog on northern Virginia's tortuous, ankle-busting "Roller Coaster." There is also everything in between: broad fire roads, rocky ledges, country lanes, rock-strewn wilderness, a stretch of U.S. 52, boulder fields, tunnels of rhododendron, stairs, bridges, wetlands, and meadows—both high and low.

Along its entire course, the AT twice exceeds 6,000 feet in elevation, at Kuwohi (also known as Clingman's Dome) in the Smoky Mountains of North Carolina and much farther north in the Presidential Range of New Hampshire. The trail dips to its lowest point, just over 100 feet above sea level, at a bridge crossing the Hudson River in New York. Needless to say, there's a lot of up and down, so much so that an end-to-end hiker will ascend and descend the equivalent of sixteen Mount Everests![2]

The AT of the Virginias is no exception. Precious little is level. In a typical twenty-five-mile section-hike, one can expect to climb at least a mile and descend by an equal amount, for an average gradient of eight percent. Most of the AT in the Virginias is well graded, and switchbacks tame steep ascents, limiting most grades to about ten percent, a foot of rise for every ten feet of horizontal distance.

The greatest continuous ascent/descent within the Virginias lies in the Tye River watershed of Nelson and Amherst Counties. Heading south from the 4,000-foot summit of Three Ridges, one descends to the Tye River, 1,000 feet above sea level, only to regain the entire half-mile-plus vertical loss in a continuous climb to the summit of The Priest. Along the four-mile trail up The Priest, the gradient is a taxing 750 feet per mile, almost fifteen percent, but, mercifully, is nearly constant the whole way.

There are, however, here and there in Virginia, scattered stretches of trail with gradients as high as twenty percent, and on these sections one curses the trail blazer. Thankfully, most are short. Steep uphill is hard on the heart and lungs. Steep downhill is worse: treacherous. It's murder on the knees and rife with opportunity for a tumble, particularly when the trail is wet or the hiker exhausted. Most AT thru-hikers are four-footed creatures, relying on two hiking poles. I'm told by an orthopedist this reduces stress on the knees by thirty percent.

Two of the most tormenting sections of the AT that I've hiked, however, were nearly flat boulder fields: a section north of Reeds Gap along the upper Blue Ridge Parkway and another north of Bailey Gap Shelter and south of Mountain Lake Wilderness. Above Bailey Gap the AT traverses across more than a mile of large, moss-encrusted stones through an utterly primeval forest. Loose stones, which are abundant, tilt disconcertingly under the hiker's weight. The boulder field at Reeds Gap is not nearly so long, but I hiked it after days of rain had rendered the stones perilously slick. The concentration necessary to avoid a spill was so vexing that, upon arriving safely at my car, I immediately developed a migraine.

It's not all ordeal by any means. At the other extreme are the meadows where footing is easy, views superb, and open expanse a welcome relief after days in dark forest.

Occasionally, one stumbles upon a rare flat section of trail. Just north of Teas near Sugar Grove, the AT follows an old logging railroad bed for more than a mile. Flat walking at three miles per hour on a dirt trail that's easy on the feet: sheer bliss at the end of a hard day.

Speaking of hiking bliss, consider the plentiful rhododendron tunnels. These usually follow alongside creeks, where the trail is relatively flat and the air cool even on sultry summer days. Along Dismal Creek south of Pearis Mountain, for example, there are nearly continuous rhododendron tunnels for perhaps three miles. Even in August the hiking was pleasant. Another rhododendron tunnel I recall was just a few yards long, though memorable for an entirely different reason. A mile or so south of the Visitor Center of Mount Rogers National Recreation Area is a short tunnel so deeply shaded that I contemplated pulling out my headlamp at eleven in the morning.

By and large the AT sticks to the spine of the Appalachians, and that's true in the Virginias as well. A day's journey is often rewarded by a handful of spectacular views from rock outcrops. Such ecstasy more than compensates for the agony of getting there.

The maximum elevation on the AT in the Virginias, roughly 5,500 feet, occurs not surprisingly near Mount Rogers's 5,729-feet summit, the highest point of the Old Dominion. Uncharacteristically, the AT bypasses the summit, from which there is no view. A side trail leads to the summit for the diehard hiker. The lowest point of the AT in the Virginias, 246 feet above sea level, is along the railroad bridge that crosses the Potomac

This signpost on the AT 3.5 miles (5.6 kilometers) south of Damascus, Virginia, marks the Virginia/Tennessee state line. The boundary also delineates Mount Rogers National Recreation Area to the north and Cherokee National Forest to the south.

Most AT blazes are painted on trees, but here the rocks guide the way along open Wilburn Ridge in Mount Rogers National Recreation Area. The dominant peak in the distance, in this view toward the south, is most likely North Carolina's Phoenix Mountain (elevation 4,710 feet/1,436 meters). (Also, see page 61, top.)

A double blaze at Tinker Cliffs alerts hikers that the AT hugs precipitous ledges at this location. (Also, see page 59.)

River at Harpers Ferry, West Virginia. In between these highest and lowest points, the AT tops many peaks but also dips to a mere 654 feet above sea level at the pedestrian bridge over the James River near Glasgow, Virginia.

For the AT's entire 2,197.4-mile length, rectangular white paint blazes—little lighthouses five inches high by one-and-one-half inches wide—guide hikers' footsteps. Blazes appear mostly on trees, sometimes on rocks, infrequently on posts. Occasional double blazes signify "Heads-up. Pay attention!" Something is about to change: usually the trail's direction, for instance, via a switchback. Side trails, such as the one to Mount Rogers, are marked similarly, with blue blazes.[3] Could this be the origin of "Where in the blue blazes am I?"

The AT's unsung heroes are the volunteer maintenance crews that keep trails marked, pathways cleared, washouts rare, and signs up-to-date. They also maintain the three-sided shelters interspersed every ten to fifteen miles along the route. In Virginia, a plethora of regional AT clubs perform these services: Potomac Appalachian Trail Club, Old Dominion

TOP: Like tiny lighthouses, one-and-one-half by five-inch (3.8 by 12.7 centimeters) white blazes guide AT hikers for its 2,197.4 miles (3,536 kilometers).
BOTTOM: Near Rhododendron Gap (elevation 5,526 feet/1,684 meters) trees are spindly.

On the AT in the Virginias, hikers will encounter sections that are dirt, gravel, or paved; grassy or mossy; rocky or boulder-strewn, like this section on the eastern flank of Peters Mountain, a ridge whose fifty-two miles (83.7 kilometers) skirt the Virginia/West Virginia border.

ATC, Tidewater ATC, Natural Bridge ATC, Outdoor Club of Virginia Tech, Roanoke ATC, Piedmont AT Hikers, Konnarock Trail Crew, and Mount Rogers ATC. By far the largest is the PATC, given the trail's proximity to the greater Washington, D.C., area. At the peak of the hiking season, some trail clubs also employ a few "ridgerunners," seasonal rangers whose job is to care for both the travelers and the trail should something out-of-the-ordinary arise. I encountered two helpful ridgerunners of the Roanoke ATC on section-hikes south of Daleville, Virginia.

Serendipitously, in September 2017, I met Homer Witcher, a legendary AT volunteer. Fatigue and my fear of edges had resulted in a decision to bypass temporarily a particularly challenging section of trail immediately north of Dragons Tooth.[4] Initially inclined to call it a day, I'd met a kindly ridgerunner on a spur trail to the closest parking lot. Somehow his encouragement inspired Plan B: Bum a ride back to my car, skip the troublesome section for now, and continue hiking south at the northern entrance to Brush Mountain

TOP: Although this stepped section on Garden Mountain near Walker Gap is not flagged on trail maps or apps, the author could not help but dub it "Stairway to Heaven."

BOTTOM: At the summit of Glade Mountain, the AT is decidedly rocky. Hikers need to take care navigating such "rock gardens" in order not to fall or turn an ankle. For this reason, the author relied consistently on a pole and premier hiking boots with substantial ankle support.

OPPOSITE: Through a primeval forest north of Bailey Gap Shelter, the AT negotiates a mile (1.6 kilometers) or more of a treacherous boulder field. Hikers must take great care walking in such terrain.

Wilderness. Even with GPS, getting to the new point of access was an adventure that involved winding back roads, a mile or two on a primitive dirt road, and the ford of a rocky creek in my car, praying I'd not get stuck. Oh, and how was I to retrieve my car in such a remote location at the end of the section? Hell's bells, worry about that when the time comes.

Late in the afternoon a day or two later, on a southbound climb to the Eastern Continental Divide, I met a northbound solo section-hiker from Norfolk, Virginia. Like me he was nibbling away sections of trail on weekends, about one per month. I enquired about how he planned to retrieve his car at the end of the section. "Oh, I called Homer," he said, and gave me Homer's number, which I stored in my phone. At a high point on the ridge where one or two bars of cell reception kicked in, I called Homer. He answered immediately and agreed to meet me in a few hours at VA 42. He did, and, on the drive back to my car, his story spilled out.

Homer married relatively late in life, in a simple ceremony at McAfee Knob, a spectacular and popular rock outcrop on the AT near Roanoke (see page 55, top). A few years later, at the insistence of his much younger wife, Homer left a lucrative but stressful job in hospital administration. "Your job is going to kill you," his wife said. "We're hiking the AT as a family." They'd already accomplished several hundred miles of the trail by sections, so Homer presumed they'd pick up where they'd left off. Not so. His wife wanted to start from scratch and thru-hike the whole enchilada. They did, parents and two teenagers, daughter and son. They completed the thru-hike without mishap, thriving individually and as a family. Today, for the sheer love of it, the family foursome maintains 120 miles of trail and sixteen trail shelters. Now pushing eighty, Homer's a professional trail angel. When I met him, he'd just run his first marathon. Homer never returned to hospital administration. Thank goodness for me and hundreds of other hikers in need of an angel.

In October 2021, the world celebrated the centennial anniversary of the conception of the Appalachian Trail, first proposed in October 1921 by Benton MacKaye (1879–1975). He floated the idea originally from an unlikely pulpit: the *Journal of the American Institute of Architects*. A New-England-bred forester, conservationist, planner, and educator, MacKaye was also a visionary. In reading his tightly argued essay, "An Appalachian Trail: A Project in Regional Planning," one wonders if he weren't also a prophet who could peer deeply into the soul of America, including its dark places.[5]

In MacKaye's words, 1921 was a time of "general upheaval."[6] The world had barely survived a conflagration of war that, in retrospect, was senseless. Economies around the globe reeled from simultaneous high inflation and unemployment. Rapid industrialization had exposed the excesses of capitalism: sweat shops, greed, belching smokestacks. By 1920, massive demographic changes in the U.S. had shifted the nation from primarily rural to predominantly urban. Each way of life had its pros and cons. Rural living fostered self-reliance at the price of a certain loneliness and cultural deprivation. Urban living provided educational and cultural opportunities at the expense of polluted atmosphere and the stress of a hectic and consumptive lifestyle. Today's red/blue political polarization has its roots in the different values and needs of rural and urban communities. But then, as now, the fundamental problem of living for all was the same: economic survival.

MacKaye's vision was radical: It sought to simultaneously address many societal ills. First and foremost, civilization had divorced humanity from nature and rendered us as "helpless as canaries in a cage."[7] Today, I suppose we'd say that civilized living has turned

TOP: From Daleville, Virginia, SOBO hikers encounter stunning rock formations in rapid succession: Hay Rock (shown here) followed by the "Triple Crown" of Tinker Cliffs (page 59), McAfee Knob (page 55, top), and Dragons Tooth (page 60).
BOTTOM: A bizarre rock mound marks the junction of the AT and the Andy Lane Trail at Scorched Earth Gap (elevation 3,197 feet/974 meters).

TOP: In central Virginia, the AT often follows closely the Skyline Drive and Blue Ridge Parkway, snuggling here against a parkway wall built by the CCC (Civilian Conservation Corps).
BOTTOM: The proximity of the AT to the Skyline Drive and Blue Ridge Parkway affords amenities to hikers such as access to picnic grounds. Here, a short side trail leads to a parkway picnic area.

us into snowflakes. Modern Americans, both rural and urban, needed the conveniences of progress but "without its puniness."[8] What better way to regain physical and mental vigor than to immerse oneself in nature for extended periods? Time in nature afforded many amenities: recreation, health and recuperation, new perspective. And labor-saving devices, already born or on the horizon, promised to reduce life's drudgery and afford common folk more leisure time. What better way to invest one's newfound leisure than surrounded by nature?

To reach the most Americans, MacKaye's proposal suggested that recreational camps be located near population centers. Most of the eastern U.S., however, with its high population density, was already heavily developed; that is, save for the spine of the Appalachian range. It was there he proposed to locate a chain of camps.

MacKaye envisioned four chief aspects of his "Appalachian Project": a trail; shelter camps; community camps; and food, farm, and forestry camps. The original trail proposal was ambitious: It called for a continuous footpath from Mount Washington in New Hampshire's White Mountains to Mount Mitchell in North Carolina's Great Smoky Mountains. In between, the trail would visit the wilds of the Adirondacks, Green Mountains, Berkshires, Catskills, Alleghenies, and Blue Ridge Mountains. The trail was to be constructed in sections, each assigned to a local community responsible for its preservation and maintenance. A good many sections already existed; for example, the 210-mile "Long Trail" through Vermont's Green Mountains. Much of the AT could be completed simply by connecting existing trails.

MacKaye conceived of shelter camps, too: a string of Swiss-style chalets, located at intervals so that the distance between camps was a "comfortable day's walk."[9] At some shelter camps, inns and semi-permanent community camps would organically spring up. These communities were envisioned primarily to serve educational purposes. Finally, there would be a few food, farm, and forestry camps to provide for logistical needs of the trail community. Although MacKaye didn't say so explicitly, one senses a longing that farm camps could build a genuine sense of community among urban and rural folks. The city slickers could benefit from getting back to the land under the guidance of rural folk, and the "hayseeds" could expand their world-views from contact with urban folk. For all, he hoped for a "retreat from profit. Cooperation replaces antagonism, trust replaces suspicion, emulation replaces competition."[10]

Participants in MacKaye's Appalachian Project were never intended to be mere spectators. Life in a recreational camp was as a volunteer worker, fully contributing to the needs of the community and the nation while benefitting oneself by physical exertion, fresh air, and a change of perspective. MacKaye calculated that there was enough leisure time in the U.S. in 1921 to keep the camps staffed year-round with a complement of 40,000.

TOP: Double blazes on the AT alert hikers to upcoming changes that warrant attention, for example, to avoid this false trail south of Tinker Cliffs (see page 59).

BOTTOM: Late spring is a grand time for hiking mountain trails, many of which, like the AT, are festooned at that time of year with mountain laurel in bloom. Note the large fallen oak tree on the left.

TOP: This weather-beaten trail sign on the AT attests to the harsh climate on Apple Orchard Mountain, near the high point (3,944 feet/1,202 meters) of the Blue Ridge Parkway in Virginia. **BOTTOM**: On Apple Orchard Mountain (4,222 feet/1,287 meters), where weather can be harsh, fog partly obscures an FAA radar dome, originally part of the nation's Distant Early Warning (DEW) line against ballistic missiles.[11] The meadow's delicate wildflowers, unlike the hiker who admired them, seem unconcerned as to DEW-line's mission: to deter nuclear warfare.

This attention-grabbing passageway on Apple Orchard Mountain is known affectionately as the "Guillotine." In glacially sculpted mountains such as the Rockies, one often finds randomly deposited boulders known as "glacial erratics." But in the Southern Appalachians, beyond the reaches of the last Ice Age, it stretches the imagination to explain the placement of the boulder in the "Guillotine."

Admittedly, the vision was utopian. And, truth be told, MacKaye was as much a dreamer as a doer. Without the organizational skills of two movers and shakers, the AT would have been stillborn. The first was Arthur Perkins (1864–1932), a prominent lawyer and judge of Hartford, Connecticut. Appointed chairman of the ATC in 1928, "Judge Perkins roamed up and down the trail corridor, enlisting workers, forming Appalachian Trail Clubs, and plotting specific routes."[12] The second was Myron Avery (1899–1952), a twenty-seven-year-old maritime lawyer who, at the encouragement of Perkins, organized the Potomac Appalachian Trail Club in 1927. When illness incapacitated Perkins, Avery took the reins of the ATC, a position he held for twenty-two years. It was on Avery's watch that the AT was completed in 1937. As Guy and Laura Waterman write:

> If Benton was indispensable to the creation of the Appalachian Trail, so was Myron Halliburton Avery. Two less compatible characters could scarcely be conjured. It is not surprising that they did not get along. Against MacKaye's rambling, pipe-smoking, airy visions, Avery displayed pragmatic, no-nonsense dedication to results.[13]

And yet it's remarkable how much of MacKaye's vision survives. Nearly ninety years since its completion in 1937, dozens of regional trail clubs maintain the AT, just as MacKaye envisioned. There are 260 trail shelters on the AT, spaced at an average interval of 8.5 miles, a "comfortable" day's journey for most hikers. Inns and lodges have sprung up here and there, also as MacKaye anticipated. In Virginia, for example, along the Skyline Drive in Shenandoah National Park sit rustic Skyland and Big Meadows Lodges, and along the Blue Ridge Parkway there's Peaks of Otter Lodge (see page 114). These two scenic drives also offer a number of waysides featuring visitor centers, analogous to the educational communities foreseen by MacKaye. One can't help but wonder if MacKaye's notion of the recreational camp directly or indirectly inspired President Franklin Delano Roosevelt's creation of the Civilian Conservation Corps (CCC), for many national and state parks originated during the Great Depression. Their infrastructure was largely built by the CCC, which provided meaningful work for unemployed, unmarried men from 1933 until America entered World War II in 1942. Finally, MacKaye's rich legacy also includes co-founding the Wilderness Society in 1935, along with iconic conservationist Aldo Leopold. Since its founding, the Wilderness Society has protected more than 111 million acres of America's most pristine wild areas. In Virginia alone, the AT runs through at least nine designated wilderness areas.

In 1921, when the AT was but a twinkle in MacKaye's eye, the U.S. had just over 100 million inhabitants. Today's population is nearly three and a half times that. MacKaye hoped that the benefits of his recreational camps might reach all or most quarters of American society, including those without access to wild nature. In that regard, he was

There are sections of the AT in Virginia so remote that no signs of human habitation are visible: only rocks, sky, and wilderness. As Henry David Thoreau conveyed in his seminal essay, "Walking" (1862): "In wildness is the preservation of the world."[14]

overly optimistic. Still, it's hard to overestimate the positive ripple effects, at both a national and international level, of MacKaye's inspired vision for the AT in 1921.

The AT that MacKaye, Perkins, and Avery breathed into life is a living organism, not an immutable pathway. In 1958, for example, its origin in Georgia shifted twenty miles from Mount Oglethorpe to Springer Mountain, a move necessitated by overdevelopment near the original terminus.[15] Repairs due to overuse, changing rights-of-way, and rerouting to make water more accessible are among the reasons the AT keeps shape-shifting. Today an AT hiker will tread a different pathway from the one of yesteryear, especially in Virginia, where 300 miles of trail, much of it "obliterated" by the Blue Ridge Parkway, were shifted fifty miles to the west in 1952, as detailed in Mills Kelly's *Virginia's Lost Appalachian Trail* (2023).[16]

Whichever AT you hike, expect adventure. Follow the blazes. Off we go!

On Wilburn Ridge, AT hikers must negotiate "Fat Man's Squeeze," so named by them for obvious reasons. (Also, see page 30.)

The "Postman," a southbound (SOBO) "flip-flopper" whom the author met one morning south of Trimpi Shelter. Because the author was headed northbound (NOBO), Postman thanked him, with a twinkle, for clearing the cobwebs along his path.

TWO

Hikers

I was no longer following a trail.
I was learning to follow myself.[1]

—ASPEN MATIS

I ENJOY SOLITUDE AND MOST OFTEN HIKE SOLO. Still, it's a joy to encounter other hikers, to hear another's story. On the AT, one meets day-hikers, section-hikers, and thru-hikers. Motivations and personalities differ.

Thru-hikers complete the entire AT in one continuous walk of four to six months or more. Of the some 3,000 people who annually set out on a thru-hike, only twenty to twenty-five percent finish it.[2] If you've never attempted a multiple-day trail hike with a load, you can't imagine how arduous the task.

The demographic distribution of thru-hikers is distinctly bi-modal. There are the young in their twenties who haven't started careers, and there are retirees like me in our fifties and sixties—or even seventies—with time on our hands. There are precious few in between.

I'm a section-hiker. I nibble off only twenty to thirty-five miles at a stretch of two to four days. And I typically travel southbound. Most thru-hikers are NOBOs; that is, north-bounders. As a solo hiker traveling against the flow, I meet more fellow hikers than if I were to trek northbound. This affords some peace of mind were I to get into serious trouble from accident or illness. For logistical reasons, I reversed the trend on two section-hikes. In three and one-half days of NOBO hiking on Pearis Mountain, I met no other hikers, except at Woods Hole Hostel. And in the off-season, even hiking SOBO, human encounters can be so rare that passing hikers are tempted to hug.

Over these many seasons of section-hiking, I've developed some impressions of thru-hikers. They pass in waves. The young, fit, and gregarious head north from Springer Mountain, Georgia, in late February or early March. They boogey, often knocking off twenty to twenty-four miles a day (whereas the average is seventeen). Their wave crests near Roanoke, Virginia, in May. The last time I camped near a trail shelter during peak thru-hiking season, I shared the area with about twenty-five of them. It was hard to find a spot on the ground, even for a two-foot by seven-foot tent. This bunch was rowdy and profane. I'm no prude, but the constant F-bombs grated on me when sitting at a picnic table in pristine woods. Still, these guys and almost as many gals looked after one another, so not a bad lot after all.

The older thru-hikers—and the more introverted ones, young or old—come in the second wave. They tend to start later, in March or April, to avoid the mobs of the first wave, and they pass through central Virginia late in the month of June. I confess: These are my kindred spirits. They're not as likely to be burning up the trail. They'll stop, make small talk, give you tips, and most of all warm you with a smile.

On the last day of a section-hike in 2016, I encountered "Rusty" resting on a rock during a water break. He looked to be about fifty, with a lean build, a bandana, and longish gray hair. We were headed in opposite directions, so I asked him if the trail to the south crossed the Blue Ridge Parkway. I was due to meet Suzanne, my wife, at milepost 75 around three in the afternoon. My trail map was inconclusive about whether the Parkway and footpath physically crossed or were only proximate. Rusty happily opened the AT app on his phone to address my concerns. It revealed that, although the road and the trail did not quite cross, they were just yards apart, rather than miles, at the rendezvous point. As Rusty navigated the iPhone with dexterity, I noticed his malformed hands and that he sometimes used a knuckle to tap the screen. I couldn't help but wonder if his feet were similarly afflicted and how that might affect long-distance travels by foot. I didn't ask, of course. Still, something exchanged in both the silences and the words between us, and I felt a kinship. On that day I met several like Rusty, each a kind soul, a lover of "the haunts of Nature."[3]

Three years previously, at a trail shelter, I had met two brothers from Pennsylvania whom I still recall with fondness, though I cannot summon their names. The older brother, then over sixty, was a warmed-over hippy who'd hiked half the AT, north to south, in his twenties. He'd stopped at Harpers Ferry and had longed ever since to complete the trail's southern half. The brother, a few years younger, was an engineer in a titanium manufacturing plant. He'd lost several ribs to childhood cancer, but he'd survived and stayed fit. The older brother had talked the younger one into section-hiking the not-yet-completed lower half of the AT, biting off a sizable chunk each summer. The brothers were clearly close, and they readily took me in. I camped with them one evening and hung with them for most of the next day, but we parted when my daily mileage limitation required me to stop.

The kindly brothers were well-provisioned and well-prepared. They were the first to introduce me to an ultraviolet SteriPEN for water purification. I now use one religiously. Impressively, they'd freeze-dried their own camp food and processed their own beef jerky. Like most distance hikers, forced to jettison every non-essential ounce to shrink the

TOP: Swiss thru-hiker "CH" and another wayfarer take a brief respite at Bailey Gap Shelter. **BOTTOM**: Hikers, hostelers, and friends enjoy a home-cooked organic dinner at Woods Hole Hostel on Pearis Mountain (highest elevation 3,770 feet/1,149 meters).

TOP: Day-hikers Jeff Heie and Tammy Krause, with four-legged companions Edy and Roo, experience the remote Henry Lanum Loop Trail for the first time.
BOTTOM: Suzanne, my wife, stands with an international cadre of humanitarian "de-miners" on an outing at the popular Hawksbill Summit overlook (4,050 feet/1,234 meters) in Shenandoah National Park with its 360-degree views. These landmine remediation supervisors from around the globe were in Virginia to learn best-managerial practices at nearby James Madison University.

ever-oppressive load, they'd realized they were over-provisioned and offered me a pack of jerky. It was the best I've ever eaten, better even than that from the Whisky River Jerky Shoppe at the Mennonite market in Dayton, Virginia. I sure hope those guys are nearing Springer Mountain by now. They so deserve to finish and celebrate.

Each passing year brings more "vintage" hikers onto the trail. With the publication of Ben Montgomery's *Grandma Gatewood's Walk: The Inspiring Story of the Woman Who Saved the Appalachian Trail* (Chicago Review Press, 2014), the numbers of older hikers will likely continue to swell. If you haven't yet heard the story, Emma Gatewood was among the first women to thru-hike the AT, completing it in 1955 at sixty-seven years of age. The mother of eleven and grandmother of twenty-three, Grandma Gatewood carried her primitive equipment in a sack slung over a shoulder. The very next year she thru-hiked the AT again. Then, for good measure, she section-hiked the entire trail the year after that.

Not all thru-hikers are NOBOs. A rare few hike southbound (SOBO) the entire way. A more popular variant, though, is the flip-flop hike. The typical flip-flop traverse is from Harpers Ferry north to Mount Katahdin, followed by Harpers Ferry south to Springer Mountain. Flip-flopping has distinct advantages, particularly if one prefers relative solitude. It avoids backcountry overcrowding associated with the NOBO waves. Moreover, one starts with milder terrain than Georgia's killer: Springer Mountain. And, finally, one can take better advantage of the seasons to avoid some of the weather extremes experienced by NOBOs.

A relatively recent trend is encountering more and more hikers from other countries on the AT. Aussies and Kiwis are well known for their "walkabouts," but recently I've met Brits and Scots as well as Irish, German, Swiss, Chinese, and Israeli thru-hikers. The word keeps leaking out to the world of the natural treasure that is America's AT.

Thru-hikers tend to congregate into small, short-lived groups called "bubbles." Distance backpacking is exceedingly strenuous, so taxing that each trekker must follow his or her or their own drummer. Consequently, bubbles, appropriately named, are fleeting. Three to five hikers may trek together for a few hundred miles, but individual constraints—injuries, "zero days" for rest and re-supply, outside commitments—soon burst a bubble. No problem. Another congenial bubble will likely form.

Truth be told, not all hikers but many—like Grandma Gatewood—hike the trail to tame demons or to heal some inner trauma: a broken relationship, substance abuse, PTSD, eating disorders, negative parental expectations, low self-esteem. Emma Gatewood's husband was abusive; long walks in the woods offered respites from his rages and physical abuse. Earl Shaffer, the AT's first thru-hiker and a World War II veteran, hiked the AT in 1948 to shake off wartime trauma. Several years ago, I met a father-and-son duo who section-hiked 100 miles or so each summer. Without prodding, the father volunteered how the tradition started: as therapy for his alcoholism. By all appearances,

TOP: In a 2,000-foot (610-meter) descent from Chestnut Knob, a SOBO hiker first follows a rock-slabbed fire road, then this grassy trail, then meadows that stretch for two miles (3.2 kilometers), and finally forest, bottoming out at a creek.
BOTTOM: This small but scenic footbridge spans Lynn Camp Creek north of Ceres, Virginia. The author camped near here in August 2019, the night before competing his last major section of the AT in the Virginias. For hikers confronting Lynn Camp Creek's steep gully, this bridge is a welcome sight.

TOP: Livestock gates, such as this one south of Wise Shelter, allow hikers and their pets to pass but restrict access by horses and cattle.
BOTTOM: The effectiveness of modern livestock gates, such as this one in Mount Rogers National Recreation Area, north of Scales, Virginia, depends on hikers responsibly closing gates behind them.

including the obvious father-son bond, the AT therapy was working its magic. Given a chance, nature can mend the hearts of us all.

Thru-hikers assume trail names, losing their given names and non-trail identities. A trail name, I suppose, offers a judicious blend of familiarity and anonymity. No one signs the log book at a trail shelter with their given name, and, when you meet another hiker, you ask only for a trail name. Some trail names—say, "Montana"—associate the hiker with where they're from. Others get identified with an item of gear or clothing, say, "Bandana." Most earn their trail name from some random event on the trail that seems a defining experience. The AT thru-hiker register of 2015 featured "Wistful," "June Bug," "BonBon," and "Dream Catcher," among hundreds of others. The memorial AT "Foot" Bridge over the James River is so named, tongue-in-cheek, for William Foot, a dedicated AT maintainer and promoter, now deceased. He and his wife, both thru-hikers, were collectively "The Happy Feet."

I've forgotten most of the trail names of those encountered, but among those remembered are the long-haired, helpful "Rusty," "Ramble On Rose," and "Madeira." A forty-ish woman, "Madiera," was thru-hiking the entire AT a second time, this time trip with faithful companion, "Ramble On Rose." A Swiss hiker I encountered at the Bailey Gap shelter went by the trail name "CH," also a bit of a pun. The initials of his given name, which I've forgotten, were C. H. But CH also appears on the European license plates of citizens of Switzerland, officially the Confederation of Helvetia. Oh, yeah, and then there was "Santa," a sixty-something fellow bounding up the trail in a red-and-white Santa hat. It takes all kinds.

The AT is not only a trail. It is a linear community numbering into the tens of thousands. And that community is comprised not just of hikers. It's an entire ecosystem that includes hikers, staff of the Appalachian Trail Conservancy, an all-volunteer army of trail maintainers, and a heavenly host of "trail angels" engaged in all manner of random acts of kindness.

Hiking the AT can be and often is a solitary adventure, but that adventure could not happen without the unsung contributions of thousands of people and nonprofit organizations such as the ATC and Potomac Appalachian Trail Club. It takes a community and a commitment to the public good.

OPPOSITE TOP: The author's daughter, Elena, de-stressing at McAfee Knob the day prior to sitting for the 2022 Virginia Bar Exam in Roanoke, Virginia. McAfee Knob, a cantilevered rock outcrop with exquisite views and a popular day-hike destination, is the "most photographed spot on the entire AT."[4] Photograph by a random AT hiker using "Ellie's" iPhone.
OPPOSITE BOTTOM: A group of day-hikers enjoys unmatched views atop Wilburn Ridge in Mount Rogers National Recreation Area. This 4.4-mile (seven-kilometer) trail (round trip) is generally considered a challenging hike, but the views are worth the effort.

The contiguous states of Virginia and West Virginia share approximately ten miles (sixteen kilometers) of the AT along Peters Mountain, a fifty-two-mile-long ridge (83.7 kilometers). To the west from this clearing, near Rice Field Shelter on the mountain, one gazes toward communities in West Virginia along U.S. 219.

THREE

Vistas

Each time we thus reach out with joy, each time we cast our view toward distances that have not yet been touched, we transform not only the present moment and the one following but also alter the past within us . . . [1]

—RAINER MARIA RILKE

A GOOD DAY ON THE AT affords two or three soul-altering vistas. These are especially welcome when one has walked for hours, sometimes days, shrouded in dark forest.

Although I've lived most of my life in Virginia, I grew up in West Virginia and lived for a time in Arizona. The contrasts of geography are stark. My hometown of Bluefield, West Virginia, perhaps just twelve miles as the crow flies from the AT, lies on the Virginia-West Virginia border. There is one of each: a Bluefield in each state. My parents, now deceased, each came from a Bluefield: Dad from Virginia, Mom from West Virginia.

Both states are mountainous, but the topography is altogether different. On the Virginia side of the border, mountains align in parallel ridges, with valleys in-between: East River Mountain, Buckhorn Mountain, Brushy Mountain, Little Walker Mountain, Big Walker Mountain, and so on. On the West Virginia side, mountains are amorphous, like convolutions of the brain. In lieu of valleys, there are hollows. (We call them "hollers.") Hollows are dead ends, literally and figuratively. Topography influences outlook. Life in the hollows seems more circumscribed, less imbued with promise.

When I revisit my hometown in West Virginia with its nearby coalfields, I feel a subtle shift in consciousness. Opportunities and options seem to evaporate. A body feels that one must make the best of the cards one has been dealt. Don't expect a new deal. Don't complain that the deck might be stacked.

Until I moved away, I was largely unaware of the psychic tug exerted by place. The connection came to the fore in Tucson, Arizona, where I lived for four years while in graduate school. Before Tucson, I'd known a relatively sheltered life and held, admittedly, a narrow world-view. Time in the Great Sonoran Desert changed all that. I had an awakening of sorts,

From the ridges followed by the AT, a hiker is afforded many lovely vistas of verdant valleys.

albeit gradual. The world became richer, more pregnant with possibility. I traveled widely and broadened my circle of friends to include those from varied countries and perspectives.

Tucson is also a mountainous world, but the mountains there are isolated islands that protrude thousands of feet from the surrounding desert. From the 9,000-foot-plus summits of Mount Lemmon or Mount Wrightson, one gazes over tens of thousands of square miles of landscape. There in the desert, the sun prevails for more than 300 days per year, and the light is brilliant. Contrasts are stark, colors vivid: deep-blue sky, red rock, green vegetation, orange sunset, little shade. Little wonder that artists like Georgia O'Keefe and Ed Mell and photographers like Ansel Adams and Laura Gilpen were drawn to desert light like moths to a flame.

But I digress. What has Tucson to do with the AT, 2,500 miles to the east? Only that the outer landscape influences the inner landscape. Twenty-four astronauts journeyed to the moon during eight Apollo missions, six of which landed successfully on the lunar surface. Chosen for their Right Stuff and not their poetic prowess, several of these celestial

Looking east from Tinker Cliffs, one sees waves of Appalachian ridges. (Also, see page 31.)

pioneers had what can only be described as mystical experiences. New perspective brought new awareness. From the vantage point of the moon, spaceship Earth appeared small, fragile, exquisitely beautiful. Granted rare glimpses of their world from an alien one, these astronauts reported epiphanies: Life on our beautiful blue marble became all the more precious and troubles all the less significant.

The Appalachian woods—"lovely, dark, and deep"—soothe the soul.[2] Solitude stills the mind. Natural sounds calm the restless chatter of modern life. And, yet, days on end in the misty shade of the AT can oppress the psyche.

What better antidote than an unexpected vista? One stumbles upon a rock outcrop into brilliant sunshine or awakening dawn or gentle sunset. From a new vantage point, the world opens up. One grasps the big picture: ridge upon ridge of Appalachian wilderness as well as verdant valleys laced by country roads and populated by rustic farms. Aches, pains, and problems recede from awareness, and the hiker surrenders to the splendor and harmony of what Native Americans call the Great Mystery.

Dragons Tooth—one-third of Virginia's hiking "Triple Crown" that also includes Tinker Cliffs and McAfee Knob (see page 55, top), all in close proximity—is a popular destination for day hikers, section hikers, and thru-hikers. In the right foreground, in the V of the tree, "Lizard," a thirty-year-old thru-hiker with whom the author chatted, relishes another of the AT's many rewards.

During my college years, I worked summers as a camp counselor at a denominational boys' camp near Peaks of Otter on the Blue Ridge Parkway. At the time, I was conventionally religious. Each week a minister or missionary would visit camp to share stories from *The Holy Bible* and instruct campers in our denomination's beliefs and doctrines. From most of those campfire lessons, I recall precious little. Once, however, a National Park Service ranger, recently transferred from the desert Southwest, spoke around the campfire of the Hopi myth of creation. Spellbound, I remember to this day almost perfectly the story of how Shrike, a stupid but determined bird, found the hole in the sky to lead a beleaguered people from this troubled world to a higher and better one.

Whether it was the ranger or the story that made the telling so indelible, I know not. But I have come to realize that there is wisdom in a worldview that respects Earth as our mother, the sky as our father, the creatures and plants as our brothers and sisters, and even the rocks as kin.

TOP: One feels atop the world in the uplands of Grayson Highlands State Park, where all the distant peaks in this view are at lower elevations.
BOTTOM: From this clearing on the AT, one sees two of Peaks of Otter's distant three summits: Sharp Top (top center) and Flat Top (top left). Not pictured is Harkening Hill.

TOP: Distant Walker Mountain is seen from an overlook on Glade Mountain, south of Atkins, Virginia.
BOTTOM: At no point on the AT in the Virginias do views surpass those of the high country near mile-high Rhododendron Gap in Mount Rogers National Recreation Area, where the trail wanders in an open meadow with expansive vistas.

TOP: Carvins Cove Natural Reserve, which borders fourteen miles (22.5 kilometers) of the AT and contains a reservoir serving the Roanoke, Virginia, area, is an outdoor enthusiast's paradise and the second-largest municipal park in the nation.
BOTTOM: By the time the Potomac River is joined by the Shenandoah River at Harpers Ferry, West Virginia (see page 76), it has become a wide flow. From this overlook, the Allegheny Mountains are visible in the distance.

A charming mid-spring view looking toward Catawba, Virginia, from the Ledges (elevation 3,000 feet/914 meters) and just three-tenths of a mile (.5 kilometer) south of the popular rock formation aptly named Dragons Tooth (see page 60).

Now, having lived almost three decades in the Shenandoah Valley, whose most prominent landmark is the bowl-shaped brow that abruptly ends Massanutten Mountain—*Shenandoah* and *Massanutten* both being of Native-American origin—I cannot help but be aware that these are sacred lands, occupied for at least 10,000 years by dozens of Indigenous peoples, many now vanished or no longer recognized. And when walking the forests of the AT, trod for millennia by these peoples, or gazing down upon their ancestral lands, I ponder an earlier time when human beings were an integral part of nature rather than would-be masters. In the quiet moments to be found on the AT, one can almost hear these Native voices who have been all but silenced yet still speak.

TOP: The amphitheater at Loft Mountain Campground in Shenandoah National Park, on a blue-blazed spur trail three-tenths of a mile (.5 kilometer) from the AT, commands terrific views of the Shenandoah Valley, including Massanutten Mountain (distant top center) near Harrisonburg, Virginia.
BOTTOM: From the AT at Blackrock Summit in Shenandoah National Park, other talus rockfalls are visible in the foreground. The historic and beautiful Shenandoah Valley is in the background.

Trail signs to water sources are often obscure, but it's hard to miss this one on the Henry Lanum Loop Trail, named in honor of a dedicated member of the Potomac Appalachian Trail Club (PATC) who maintained forest trails.

FOUR

Water

Water, water, every where,
And all the boards did shrink;
Water, water, every where,
Nor any drop to drink.[1]

—SAMUEL TAYLOR COLERIDGE

WATER AND WEATHER are never far from a hiker's mind.

Water comprises about sixty percent of the make-up of an adult male, a bit less for an adult female. Physical and mental processes deteriorate with moderate dehydration; that is, if the body's water fraction dips by ten percent. Death can occur at a deficit of twenty percent.

Fortunately, water is relatively plentiful on the AT, where springs, rivulets, brooks, creeks, and occasional falls abound. South of Wise Shelter is a section of trail crossed by no less than six small streams in a stretch of no more than 200 yards. Just north of the shelter, in a bowl surrounded by peaks, four significant streams converge almost simultaneously. On the other hand, water sources are not equally dispersed, and it is common to find stretches of ten miles or more without water.

Figuring how much water to carry for a given section of trail is a critical calculation and getting it wrong potentially life-threatening. It's complicated. Under normal circumstances, a human needs two to three liters per day. On the AT, under extreme exertion, one needs perhaps double that amount, more in hot weather. But water, at 2.2 pounds per liter (or eight pounds per gallon), is the heaviest commodity in a hiker's pack. The trick then is to carry just enough, no more than sufficient to reach the next source, with a little reserve. In principle, the calculation is a not unlike that of a pilot assessing the amount of fuel to pump into an aircraft's tanks. Excess fuel has to be lifted needlessly, reducing efficiency. Too little and the outcome could be disastrous. One aims for the sweet spot of just enough, with reasonable margin for error in unforeseen situations. Therefore, it's crucial to know the location of the next water source and whether or not it's reliable in all sea-

Who knew that rocks could sprout water fountains like this one alongside the Loft Mountain Wayside Trail in Shenandoah National Park? Another example of trail magic.

sons. For a solo hiker, the number-one utility of trail maps and apps is how they pinpoint dependable sources of water. Even so, whenever I encounter hikers on the trail, a frequent question of exchange is: How far to the next water?

Typically, one finds water in the saddle between two ridges, in ravines, or on the face of a hillside, far below the ridge line. Given that shelters are often co-located with water, if one spends the night at a shelter, one most likely faces a hefty climb right out of the starting gate the next morning.

Finding water is but part of the equation. Treating it and getting it into water bottles are additional factors in the daily ritual. A small spring or rivulet may contain sufficient water but offer no pools deep enough to submerge a bottle. At such times, AT hikers can become downright clever. More than once I've encountered the engineering of a previous hiker who's used a small rock and a curled leaf to construct a tiny spigot in a scant flow otherwise inaccessible. God bless 'em.

On the AT, prudent hikers treat water primarily to prevent contracting *giardia*, a prevalent parasite. The safest water comes from springs. The most surprising one I've run across, just south of Pine Swamp Camp Shelter, gushed from beneath a small tree right

TOP: Where the AT follows mountainsides rather than ridgetops, streams such as this one are typical.
BOTTOM: Waterproof boots are advantageous in rain and also for fording small streams when conditions permit.

Stopping to gather water on the Henry Lanum Loop Trail, one can't help but notice how a small tree clings for dear life on a substantial boulder. Another small but natural wonder along the AT.

next to the trail. Some hikers, including me on a rare occasion when desperately thirsty, will drink spring water untreated, though it's not recommended.

The lower the trail sits on a mountainside, the more careful one needs to be about a water source. A low creek adjacent to a pasture is a source of last resort.

Thirty years ago, when I did my first AT solo trek, the standard method of treating water was similar to chlorination of municipal water: Add a halogen to kill a pathogen. Then it was typically two small iodine or halazone tablets per liter. The taste was bearable at first but after a few days became more and more nauseating.

For water treatment, subtracting is better than adding. Nowadays, filtering is the favored process. Modern one-tenth micron filters remove not only particulates, but virtually all bacteria and protozoa. The first backpacking filters on the market were complicated pumps, with small parts easily lost. The most popular filter today is the Sawyer, with only two parts: a plastic bag and a filter. Fill the bag with untreated water, screw the filter onto the bag, and squeeze the bag to force the water through the filter.

The year I began section-hikes, I ran into two brothers who introduced me to another great device: the SteriPEN, a battery-powered wand that uses ultraviolet light to sterilize. If a water source is really sketchy, I both filter and sterilize.

Crabtree Falls, accessed either from above by an AT spur trail near The Priest or from below via U.S. 56, is a favorite destination for day-hikers. On a hot day, soaking one's feet in a cool stream is bliss. And there's no better way to end a hard day of hiking than to be lulled to sleep by natural white noise when camped alongside a gurgling brook. Photograph by Suzanne Fiederlein and used by permission.

A mile south of Dickey Gap on VA 16, one hears Comer Falls long before one sees the cascade.

Wise Shelter in Mount Rogers National Recreation Area sits in a topographical bowl, where several boulder-laced streams converge, including this one.

The earliest method of water sterilization was, of course, boiling. It's why the British upper crust developed tea time. On the trail, boiling consumes great quantities of fuel, a practice to avoid as a general rule. But if one is heating water anyway, for tea or rice or pasta, then boiling adds another layer of security. Two years ago, at a trail shelter, though, I encountered a novice hiker who took the admonition to "boil or treat" water to a wholly new level. He'd lugged two liter-sized propane canisters to the shelter and proceeded, in two hours of effort, to boil enough water, one or two cups at a time, to fill four liter bottles. His pack was so massive and so heavy that I was not at all confident he could climb back up the hill from the shelter. He didn't seem the type to welcome a suggestion, so I held my peace. We all start as novices, and experience is a harsh but effective teacher.

Most, but not all, trail shelters are situated near a water source. More often than not, the source is a stone's throw from the shelter. Occasionally, in the case of Rice Field Shelter on Peters Mountain, by way of a counterexample, the water source is a half-mile or more steeply downhill from the shelter.

TOP: A blue-blazed spur trail from the AT leads to Hickory Ridge Campground in southwestern Virginia's Grayson Highlands State Park, and from there a red-blazed trail (not directly connected to the AT) follows Wilson Creek along its tumultuous course (see page 123).

BOTTOM: Two large rocks form a natural sluice on Wilson Creek in Grayson Highlands State Park.

Thickets of rhododendron thrive nearby streams, and their springtime blooms enhance the visual wonderland that is the AT.

These are the survival aspects of water on the AT, but it's not all about survival. To a sweaty, bug-bitten, and gritty hiker, a shower—hot or cold—is a boon that can revive flagging spirits in short order. And to stumble upon a gurgling brook or stream on a brutally hot day, halfway up a 2,000-foot climb, affords delicious joy. Soaking one's feet in an ice-cold stream can cool the entire body. Soaking one's shirt in that same water provides two hours of evaporative air-conditioning. Camping by a stream is as good as it gets, with plentiful water, ease of cleanup of mess gear and one's body, and slumbering water-music in the bargain.

Then, too, it's common to find rhododendron growing densely along streams. In the shade of a water-cooled rhododendron tunnel, it can be ten or more degrees cooler than in the open air.

In the modern Western world, we take water for granted. Not so on the AT. Every drop is precious. Literally.

The AT accesses two of the three major bridges shown in this photo from Maryland Heights, a popular lookout perched 300 feet (ninety-one meters) above the confluence of the Shenandoah (upper left) and Potomac (lower right) Rivers at Harpers Ferry, West Virginia (see pages 6 and 11). Just 2.4 miles (3.9 kilometers) after crossing from Virginia into West Virginia along the U.S. 340 bridge (top background), the AT crosses from West Virginia into Maryland on a pedestrian walkway alongside the railroad bridge (lower left). On December 21, 2019, seven cars of a CSX freight train derailed on the rail bridge, destroying a section of the AT walkway. Miraculously, no one on the train or trail was injured. The Potomac River crossing re-opened during the July 4th weekend of 2020.

FIVE

Bridges

Like a bridge over troubled water,
I will lay me down.[1]

—SIMON AND GARFUNKEL

AS THE AT MEANDERS THROUGH THE VIRGINIAS, it crosses three iconic rivers: the Potomac, Shenandoah, and James. It also crosses the lesser known but vital New River. And it crosses scores of tributaries, creeks, and rivulets as well as a few wetlands. Needless to say, bridges are necessary for the AT's unbroken continuity. Each has character all its own.

Years ago, I attended a professional conference at Oxford University and while there was housed in an attic dorm room in a residence hall at Queens College. Strolling to dinner one pleasant evening, I passed by a classical gothic hall, with arched ceiling, bell tower, and massive oaken doors flung wide. From inside wafted a choir's enchanting rendition of "Oh, Shenandoah." The beauty of song, voices, and composition stopped me dead in my tracks. All the more because they were singing of my current home: the Shenandoah Valley of Virginia.

Even the word "Shenandoah" is musical, almost certainly Native-American in origin. The meaning, however, is obscure, but one oft-cited translation is: "beautiful daughter of the stars."[2]

The Shenandoah River meets the Potomac at Harpers Ferry, West Virginia, the northern terminus of the AT section described herein. The "Y" formed at the confluence of these substantial waterways serves as the boundary separating Maryland, West Virginia, and Virginia. To my mind, Harpers Ferry has always resembled a model-train layout. It's a quaint place. Steep bluffs on the Maryland side overlook the river junction and the town, with its hillsides and steepled churches. The AT crosses from West Virginia into Maryland alongside a railroad bridge over the Potomac. There's an Amtrak station in town, frequented both by tourists and those commuting daily to and from D.C., about sixty miles away. From the bluffs above, it all looks too idyllic to be real.

A half-mile on the AT south of the Potomac bridge lies Jefferson Rock, with its captivating view—from the opposite direction—once again of the town and the confluence.

The spot is so named because it was from this vantage that Thomas Jefferson eloquently described a scene "worth a voyage across the Atlantic."[3] Here, Jefferson explains why:

> The passage of the Patowmac through the Blue Ridge is perhaps one of the most stupendous scenes in Nature. You stand on a very high point of land. On your right comes up the Shenandoah, having ranged along the foot of the mountain a hundred miles to seek a vent. On your left approaches the Patowmac in quest of a passage also. In the moment of their junction they rush together against the mountain, rend it asunder and pass off to the sea.[4]

In 1972, the Appalachian Trail Conservancy (ATC), founded in 1925, relocated its headquarters from Washington, D.C., to Harpers Ferry, West Virginia. It was a wise move. A "trail town," Harpers Ferry sits at the psychological midpoint of the AT, although the physical midpoint lies a bit farther north, in Pine Grove Furnace State Park near Gardners, Pennsylvania. The town of Harpers Ferry punctuates Virginia's 531.7 miles and affords hikers a welcome way station, with several nice eateries and ice-cream parlors, travel access, and interesting diversions.

Harpers Ferry also has a rich history, and, indeed, the riverfront area is a National Historical Park. It was there in 1859 that abolitionist John Brown launched his insurgent raid on the U.S. arsenal. (See page 196.) And there in 1865, immediately on the heels of the Civil War, Northern Baptists established Storer College as a normal school to train black teachers. Storer closed in 1955 following the U.S. Supreme Court's *Brown v. Board of Education* decision of 1954, which ruled segregated schools as unconstitutional. In 1962, the National Park Service purchased Storer College and re-purposed it as one of four national training centers.

A short blue-blazed trail runs from the ATC headquarters, along the grounds of old Storer College, and connects with the trail itself just south of Jefferson Rock. Continuing south from there, it's another mile or so along the face of a precipitous hillside to the Shenandoah. Hikers cross the iconic river on the heavily trafficked U.S. 340 bridge. Fortunately, there's a separate pedestrian walkway, but the rumble of traffic is deafening. Midway, one enters the "Old Dominion." The trail continues to follow U.S. 340 briefly beyond the bridge, then ducks under the highway to head steeply uphill into the hinterlands of Loudon County.

Much farther south, perhaps three-quarters of the distance from Harpers Ferry to North Carolina, the AT crosses the New River near the massive Celanese fiber plant in Pearisburg. From the north, hikers drop down a steep hill, with the river visible far below on the left through the trees. At the bottom, the AT follows a paved road under the four-lane U.S. 460 bridge. It then leads hikers to a pedestrian lane on the bridge's south side. A quarter-mile later, immediately on the Pearisburg side of the New, the AT heads uphill and off into the woods, taking hikers by a hidden cemetery.

TOP: The ATC's headquarters (left door) and Visitor Center (right door) are in this building on a side trail at the intersection of Washington Street and Storer College Place in Harpers Ferry, West Virginia, designated a National Historic Park in 1963.
BOTTOM: In Harpers Ferry, a short spur trail connects the ATC's headquarters and Visitor Center with the AT at Jefferson Rock, passing through the campus of historic Storer College, now the Stephen T. Mather Training Center of the National Park Service. Stephen Tyne Mather (1867–1930) was the first Director of the National Park Service from 1916–1929.

South of Wise Shelter in the high country near Mount Rogers, the AT stays soggy much of the year. Here, a primitive two-plank bridge helps keep feet dry. When creeks are swollen, however, hikers may either have to hop the rocks or remove their boots and socks to wade across—but only when conditions, personal safety, and common sense prevail.

Heading north from Wise Shelter in Mount Rogers National Recreation Area, hikers immediately cross a small but fast-moving stream on this narrow footbridge with a single wooden handrail.

Whereas the Shenandoah, Potomac, and James Rivers ultimately drain into Chesapeake Bay and the Atlantic Ocean, the New River joins the wild and scenic Gauley River near Beckley, West Virginia, to form the Kanawha, a tributary of the Ohio River, which then merges with the Mississippi River near Cairo, Illinois, and ultimately drains into the Gulf of Mexico. That the AT passes through the watersheds of both Chesapeake Bay and the Gulf of Mexico suggests that, at some point, it must pass the Eastern Continental Divide. Sure enough, the divide, on a high ridge south of Niday Shelter, is marked with a plaque.

At the other extreme of bridge preeminence is the two-log bridge, one for each foot. These modest constructions are ubiquitous on Virginia's AT. One finds them most often where rivulets have cut narrow gullies into precipitous hillsides. At other times, two-log bridges ford mud pits that form in low spots in the rainy season.

Just south of Ceres, Virginia, the AT crosses the headwaters of the Holston River. The Holston eventually gathers into an impressive flow, but here it's just a highland creek. The trail crosses the Holston via a farmer's private concrete roadway over a culvert.

This bridge between Kelly Knob (see pages 96 and 98) and Johns Creek Shelter is typical of those that cross the AT's medium-sized creeks.

As the following photographs show, throughout the AT in the Virginias bridges vary in size, strength, durability, shape, and purpose, depending on the crossing. The AT manifests a smorgasbord of moods. Its bridges reflect these moods. Wider streams require planked bridges. There is usually a log rail for support but, more often than not, to one side only. Hikers be advised: The more primitive bridges can be treacherously slippery when moss-covered and wet. Best to use caution and a hiking pole or two. If the bridge is planked, however, the poles can introduce an unexpectedly hazard: The tip of a pole can get caught in a gap between planks, throwing the hiker off balance. So it is wise to look down and plant the tip of each pole squarely on the planks.

Serious tributaries, like Big Stony and Dismal Creeks, require well-engineered pedestrian crossings. A substantial swinging bridge ferries the hiker across Dismal Creek along Virginia Route 606. The route is known by locals as the "Wilderness Road," because it follows one of two thoroughfares used by Eastern colonial-era settlers to travel to the Cumberland Gap and beyond, into Kentucky and Tennessee.

I must confess that, in culling hundreds of photographs for this volume, many of my favorites are of bridges. Why is that? I'm not entirely sure. But it seems to me that, in

TOP: The author begins a section-hike at the Dismal Creek suspension bridge on the Wilderness Road, Bland County Route 606. Photograph by Don Raines, who ferried me to the trailhead, and used by permission.
BOTTOM: Crossing Big Stony Creek in the remote reaches of Giles County, Virginia, requires a substantial footbridge high above the flood-prone water.

TOP: Rock walls flank the AT as a gateway to this long footbridge at the edge of Raccoon Branch Wilderness (see page 97, bottom).
BOTTOM: A hiker enters Hunting Camp Creek Wilderness from the north by crossing this substantial footbridge buttressed by stone foundations.

The weathering of this log footbridge in Lewis Fork Wilderness foretells of the area's harsh winters. One can appreciate the maintenance needs for such bridges along the AT.

some mysterious way, the bridges of the AT embody its wild essence more fully than any other feature. The well-worn Appalachian Mountains are among the oldest mountains on Earth. It is water that has worn them down and given them their character. Symbolically then, water links the past to the present, and bridges reflect the character of the AT, weathered by climate and time or sparkling new like a profusion of wildflowers in spring.

Then, too, bridges are symbolic of some sort of transition, from "here" to "there." From a human perspective, many of us who hike the AT are in transition. I began my odyssey shortly after retiring. Others may be between college graduation and their first job or in between jobs. A few are veterans like Earl Shaffer, a World War II vet who was the AT's first thru-hiker and offered this motivation: to "walk the war out of my system."[5] Still others may be transitioning from substance abuse to sobriety. Every bridge crossed symbolizes a successful transition of some type.

Immediately upon crossing Fox Creek on this footbridge at the eastern edge of the Lewis Fork Wilderness, the AT climbs abruptly. One of four wilderness areas lying inside the extensive Mount Rogers National Recreation Area, Lewis Fork is home to Virginia's highest peak, Mount Rogers (elevation 5,729 feet/1,746 meters), and an environment that seems otherworldly to those who have never before visited the high country of Virginia and West Virginia.

TOP: A sturdy but weathered bridge leads into a rhododendron tunnel near Jenkins Shelter.
BOTTOM: A steel cable provides the only handrail on this rickety AT footbridge.

A lengthy boardwalk though a wetland leads up to this footbridge across a stream near Interstate 81 north of Marion, Virginia. Although one would not guess it from the photo, the din of truck traffic is significant at this location, a stone's throw from I-81. As one ventures farther into the woods, road noises gradually fade beyond perception, although, depending upon terrain, it may take three to four intervening miles (five to seven kilometers) before one escapes the din.

Perhaps Virginia's proudest river is the James, which flows 348 miles from the Appalachian Mountains to Chesapeake Bay. Formed by the junction of the Cowpasture and Jackson Rivers near Clifton Forge, the James is joined by the wild and scenic Maury River at Glasgow. From there it meanders through the Blue Ridge to the city of Lynchburg and through the Piedmont to Richmond, located at the Falls of the James, a barrier to upstream travel by boat. East of Richmond lies Virginia's Tidewater. There, the James rolls lazily to enter the Chesapeake after gracing towns of colonial prominence: Jamestown, Williamsburg, and Yorktown.

For at least 10,000 years prior to the colonization of Virginia, the James River—from the fall line in Richmond to the Blue Ridge Mountains—was home to Monacan Indians, the westernmost of eleven tribes native to Virginia and recognized by the Commonwealth. The James River Monacan, mentioned in the earliest recorded histories of Virginia by John Smith, of Jamestown fame, now claim some 2,600 living descendants comprising the Monacan Nation, a federally recognized tribe in Amherst County. Virginia's most iconic geological landmark is Natural Bridge, now a state park. There, visitors can visit the reconstruction of a Monacan settlement and learn of Monacan history and culture directly from descendants of the original James River Monacan.

As far upstream as Glasgow, the James is mighty. A few miles downstream of Glasgow, the AT spans the James via an impressive foot bridge. At 623 feet in length, the James River Memorial "Foot" Bridge is the longest pedestrian bridge not only on the AT, but in the entire National Park System. Constructed in 2000 atop piers of an abandoned railroad bridge, the "Foot" Bridge is beautiful as well as functional. A plaque explains the tongue-in-cheek name. The "Foot" Bridge memorializes William Foot, an avid hiker, AT maintainer, and advocate.

For almost as long as waterways have meandered and humans have wandered, bridges have assisted those wanderings. Think Ox-ford and Cam-bridge in Merry Ole England. So, too, on the AT, where bridges mark the nexus of footprints, trail, and water.

View of the Norfolk Southern James River Bridge (top) from the AT's James River "Foot" bridge (below), which is the National Park Service's longest pedestrian bridge at 623 feet long (190 meters).

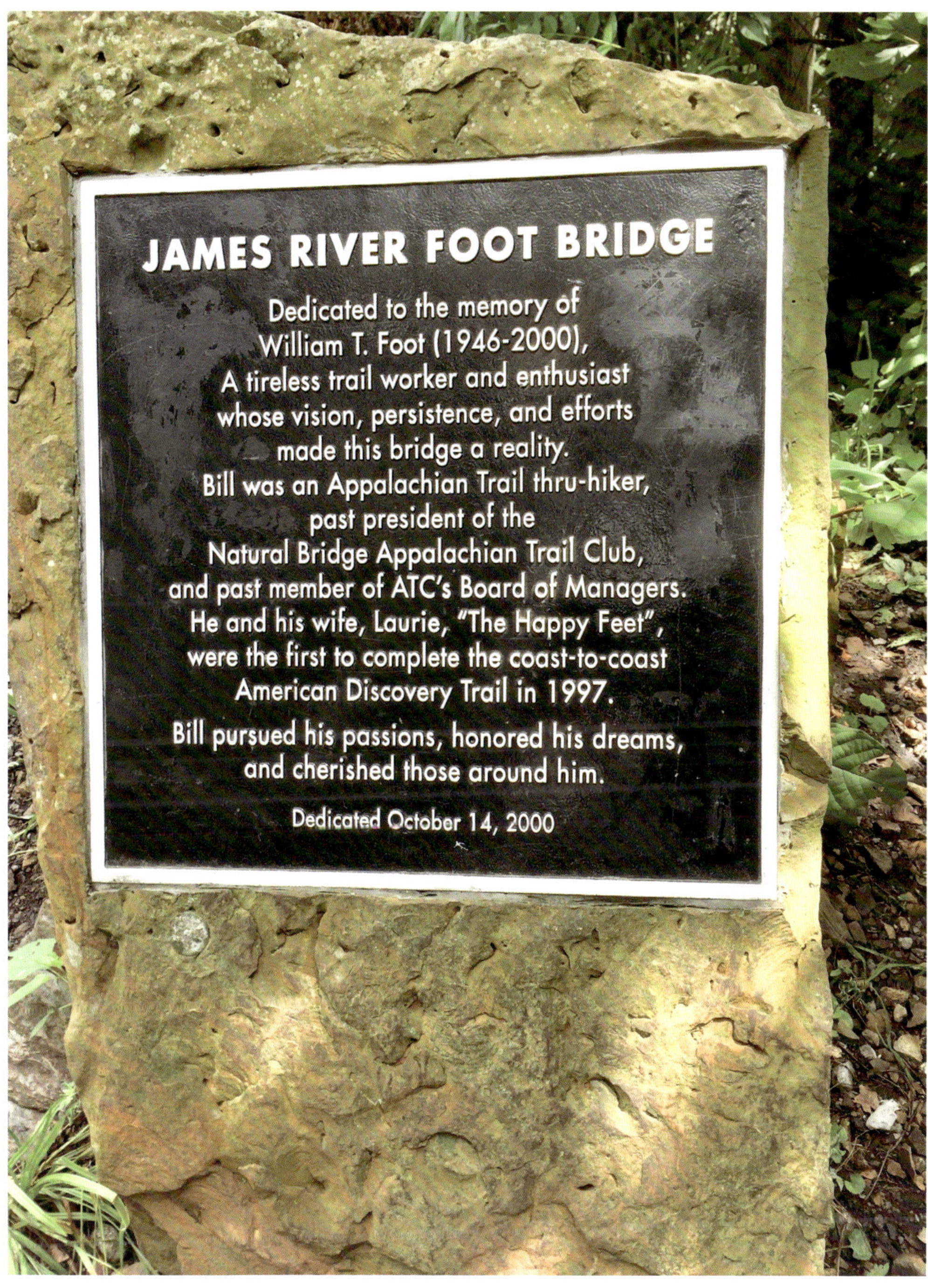

This plaque at the James River "Foot" Bridge memorializes William T. Foot for his lifetime of service to and advocacy for the AT. Photograph by Suzanne Fiederlein and used by permission.

Generally speaking hikers experience four true seasons along the AT. Yet mountains are weather incubators, and seasonal conditions can quickly turn at high elevations. In Virginia, weather in the high country of Mount Rogers National Recreation Area is unpredictable, and localized thunderstorms, like the one in the distance at right, are frequent.

SIX

Weather

A change in the weather is sufficient to recreate the whole world and ourselves.[1]

—MARCEL PROUST

WITH FEW DEVIATIONS, the AT traverses the spine of the Appalachian Mountains. The AT in the Virginias is no exception. Mountains are weather-makers, and so the hiker spends considerable time in a world of weather incubation. Anything is to be expected.

I'm a section-hiker, and, as such, I often try to time my hikes to take advantage of favorable weather. Still, it's folly not to be prepared for nature's whims. As a general rule, the higher the elevation the more mercurial the weather. A few decades ago, hypothermia took the life of a young female hiker near Mount Rogers. It was July, as I recall.

Not too long after this tragedy, during late summer, a friend and I embarked upon a three-day backpacking circuit near Grayson Highlands. We were enjoying a lovely, shirt-sleeve day, hiking at nearly 5,000 feet in elevation. A cloud blew in, the sky darkened, the temperature abruptly dropped twenty degrees, and it started to pour. My friend and I looked at each other and both uttered "Hypothermia!" in unison, as we scrambled to add layers. After bundling up and topping off with rain gear, we continued hiking in the rain. Twenty minutes later, the clouds dissipated, the sun broke out, and the temperature bounced back up to sixty-five. We peeled off the layers and, back in shirt-sleeves, began gorging on huckleberries while basking in bright sunshine.

Two decades later, in 2013, five of us sixty-something friends planned a five-day backpacking trip in Mount Rogers National Recreation Area. Bad idea: It was May. While it poured almost nonstop for three days, we tent camped in Grayson Highlands State Park, often holed up in picnic shelters, waiting for a break in the weather. At two o'clock in the afternoon of day four, the rain let up. At last, we drove to the trailhead, more than ready to hit the trail. As we strapped on packs, the wind picked up, and the skies opened with a driving rain that was nearly horizontal. We relented and raced back to shelter. An hour and a half later skies cleared; finally, we were on the trail. Two miles later the skies opened again. Our deeply rutted trail ran like a river, soaking our boots and feet. Demoralized, we turned around and tramped back to the cars. En route we met a woman thru-hiker about our age, plodding along happy as a clam in her rain gear. The next day it was clear, and three of us ventured off into the highlands, one clear day after four of nearly solid rain.

From my Boy Scout days until then, I'd always used a poncho for rain gear. Under such conditions as just described—daylong driving rains—ponchos are worse than useless. A few hours and one is drenched, body and spirit. The last Grayson Highlands experience convinced me to invest in state-of-the-art rain gear. It has saved me, or at least my spirits, more than once. The first time I used good rain gear, I sat on a log, casually cooking dinner in a downpour, every bit as dry and content as the woman hiker we'd met in a highlands squall.

Now, I'm always prepared for rain. Thunder and lightning are another story. A decade ago, a friend and I experienced an early morning thunderstorm at an overlook just off Furnace Mountain trail, a blue-blazed trail that leads from the Shenandoah Valley to Blackrock Summit (3,720 feet elevation), a stunning overlook and intriguing geological formation on the AT in Shenandoah National Park. We cowered in tents at ground zero, lightning bolts zapping all around. It was terrifying.

So I try to time section-hikes to avoid thunderstorms. It's a largely futile attempt. Mountains are weather-makers. Forecasts be damned. Two seasons ago, my only window of opportunity to hike Peters Mountain included the ominous forecast: isolated thunderstorms. What does "isolated" mean? The moment I stepped from the car after a four-hour drive to the trailhead, an "isolated" storm struck, with me as the apparent bulls-eye. I dashed back into the car. The deluge was positively torrential. Twenty minutes later, it passed. I hiked past Pine Swamp Shelter up a long climb to a wide, protected saddle. Ominous clouds blew in again. Veteran thru-hikers scrambled to set up tents in the saddle to ride out the storm. I followed suit. The storm spit a few drops, then passed. False alarm. Every day thereafter was clear.

Only once, nearly forty years ago in the Smokies, have I hiked a section of the AT in winter. The trail was snow-covered. My friend and I were well prepared, but it was too demanding to be fun and is not recommended. I've talked to several thru-hikers who trudged through March snow on the AT in North Carolina's high terrain. Not something I'd want to experience at this age.

But one needs to be prepared for winter at any time. On an Easter Sunday long ago, when I was in my twenties, Dad dropped my brother, Willie, and me on the AT near Mountain Lake Wilderness. All day we hiked the ridgeline in a freezing fog that coated every twig with half-an-inch of westward-slanting rime ice. It was as enchanting a fairyland as I've ever encountered. By midafternoon, we arrived at our destination, Bailey Gap Shelter (see page 49, top), soon to be joined by three young women, who introduced

This primitive shelter on the red-blazed Wilson Creek Trail offers minimal but welcome emergency protection from capricious storms that frequent the high country of Grayson Highlands State Park.

One of the author's most visceral memories of the AT is the considerable time spent hiking immersed in mist, fog, and cloud, as in this scene on Kelly Knob following an afternoon rain.

themselves, to our astonishment, as the Pruitt sisters! The five Pruetts/Pruitts were soon joined by five Smiths: two kids, two parents, and a dog. We'd later be thankful for the ten bodies crammed into the small shelter. By morning a gallon jug of water left on the picnic table had frozen solid. The next day, Willie and I followed the headwaters of Little Stony Creek down the eastern flank of the mountain, through a meadow, and then into the gorge that turns the creek into a sixty-five foot waterfall known as the Cascades. By the time we'd reached the outskirts of Pembroke and called Dad to retrieve us, it was a balmy sixty-five degrees Fahrenheit.

Although I am not generally a winter hiker, I find that summer can be every bit as challenging. As I've aged, heat is harder to endure than cold. With cold, one can always add another layer. With heat and water scarcity, dehydration, heat exhaustion, or heat stroke are major concerns.

Fortunately, knowing some physics helps with planning and preparation. The "adiabatic lapse rate" is three degrees Celsius per thousand feet—or equivalently about five degrees Fahrenheit. Translation: Under equilibrium conditions, atmospheric temperature

TOP: Here at an overlook on the AT near the Blue Ridge Parkway, the author is above low-hanging clouds.
BOTTOM: Early-morning mist enhances the mysterious ambience of the upper reaches of the 4,225-acre (1,710-hectare) Raccoon Branch Wilderness (see page 84, top).

At eventide on Kelly Knob, the sun finally breaks through summer rain clouds.

decreases three degrees Celsius for each 1,000 feet of elevation gain. In practical terms, if it's ninety degrees Fahrenheit in Roanoke at about 1,200 feet in elevation, it will be ten degrees Fahrenheit cooler on a nearby ridge at 3,200 feet. In actuality, it will likely be even cooler, because woods are cooler than cities, in general, and deeply shaded woods warm more slowly as the day progresses. Taking all this into account, I try to get a strenuous climb out of the way early in the morning and to be high on a ridge before the heat of day turns oppressive.

Over the past few seasons, I've hiked for days in the rain, ridden out a thunderstorm in a shelter, needed every stitch of clothing for warmth during a cold night of rain in May, and been so parched by heat that my legs cramped at night. When I reflect on all the vagaries and challenges of weather, however, one overarching image comes to mind: mist. To rise early and camp early is to spend most of the day hiking before fog and mist burn away. When one hikes thusly in the weather-making mountains followed by the AT, one is often hiking in clouds, quite literally. And when the clouds part and the sun breaks through, one might wonder, albeit fleetingly, how Moses in the *Bible* must've felt at the parting of the Red Sea.

TOP: At daybreak, fog often blankets Burke's Garden, especially during the fall.
BOTTOM: An early-morning view of Burke's Garden before the fog burns off. Burke's Garden is an oval valley ringed by Garden Mountain. (Also, see pages 182, 185, and 186.)

On a late-afternoon hike in winter, Elena ("Ellie"), the author's daughter, pauses at South River Shelter in Shenandoah National Park, one of several trail-maintenance outposts administered by the Potomac Appalachian Trail Club (PATC). (Also, see page 55, top.)

SEVEN

Shelter

Oh, a storm is threat'ning
My very life today
If I don't get some shelter
Oh yeah, I'm gonna fade away[1]

—THE ROLLING STONES

For the AT hiker, shelter is more than simply protection from the elements. It's a haven from bloodsucking insects. It's the elusive promise of respite at the end of a grueling day. It's companionship around a picnic table or campfire. It's where muscles relax, blisters get tended, and sleep "knits up the raveled sleeve of care."[2]

On the AT, shelter comes in many forms, all welcome. Most ubiquitous is the three-sided trail shelter like Rice Field Shelter on Peters Mountain (page 102, top). The classical AT shelter is of log construction with a plank floor large enough to sleep six to eight side by side. Open at front, AT shelters have large roof overhangs so that residents remain dry even in downpours. Most AT shelters sport a few nearby "amenities": a water source, picnic table, fire ring, and privy (either a pit toilet or a "moldering" one). Some shelters, such as those in Shenandoah National Park, provide bear poles: flagpole-like structures with multiple hooks where backpackers hang food out of reach of human-habituated bears. All AT shelters have a log book, the equivalent of a trail newspaper or, perhaps more accurately, a communal blog, in which hikers leave messages for fellow travelers, rant or rave about trail experiences, and engage in friendly gossip or banter.

The David Lesser Shelter is particularly memorable. Given its close proximity to D.C. and northern Virginia, it's designed for heavy traffic. The shelter itself is modern, with skylights and a huge deck complete with Adirondack chairs and a covered dining area. The area resembles a state park campground more than a typical AT shelter. There are spaces for more than a dozen tents.

Trail etiquette gives thru-hikers first dibs on shelter space. Fair enough, because some ultralight trekkers shave weight by forgoing a tent. Usually, there are a number of tent

TOP: Rice Field Shelter on Peters Mountain is of classic construction: three-sided with log walls. The steps facilitate crossing a fence along a property boundary. **BOTTOM**: Docs Knob Shelter on Pearis Mountain, of newer vintage, features framed walls and a deck with bench seating.

There's nothing like a respite at the end of a long day on the AT. Here, the author sets up camp at Punchbowl Shelter, a few tenths of a mile/kilometer off the Blue Ridge Parkway and ten miles (sixteen kilometers) north of the James River (see page 90), the next day's destination. Photograph by Suzanne Fiederlein and used by permission.

sites in proximity to the shelter for the rest of us. Many, myself included, prefer tenting to sheltering.

Standard trail shelters have some disadvantages. Being unenclosed, they don't really protect against insects. If space is no issue, I've been known to pitch my tent, minus the rain fly, inside the shelter, as protection against mosquitoes and flies. Most hikers try to be as quiet as possible, but shelters can be noisy, especially if hikers are coming and going at all hours and if there are snorers in the pack. (Alert: There are always snorers!) And with continual, sometimes heavy use, shelters become dirty and attract mice. There's been at least one confirmed case on the AT of deadly *hantavirus*, transmitted by mice. Fortunately, the hiker recovered.

Trail shelters are not all of the standard model. Newer shelters are of frame rather than log construction. A few, like Trimpi Shelter in Raccoon Branch Wilderness, are

ABOVE: Chestnut Knob Shelter (elevation 4,409 feet/1,344 meters), the former residence of a fire warden, is a rare enclosed shelter. Inside, hikers will find several bunks and a couple of picnic tables.

OPPOSITE TOP: Suzanne, the author's wife, stands outside of Partnership Shelter, near the Mount Rogers National Recreation Area's Visitor Center (see page 115, top). The shelter is atypical by being two-story and offering an attached indoor shower.

OPPOSITE BOTTOM: The stone construction of Trimpi Shelter in Raccoon Branch Wilderness is unique, offering an internal fireplace and facing bunks. Like many shelters, it lies a few tenths of a mile/kilometer off the AT on a blue-blazed spur trail.

The three-sided "moldering privy," such as this one at Knot Maul Shelter, has largely replaced pit toilets. Composting privies are more environmentally friendly than pit toilets, but they require raised platforms to house the compost. After use, hikers toss in a handful of sawdust, provided by AT volunteers in a bucket, to cover their waste and start the composting process. But stand clear if you see feet, as the privy is occupied!

constructed of stone. Trimpi's bunks face one another from the sides. Between the bunks along the back wall is a fireplace. Some, like the modern Partnership Shelter, are multi-level. A vertical ladder leads to a large loft, with open windows at each gable. Partnership Shelter even sports a shower. Its water is ice-cold, but who cares if you haven't washed in four days? There are a few enclosed trail-maintenance cabins that double as shelters. These are rare, homey luxuries.

Most serious trekkers carry ultralight tents, weighing in at two to three pounds. A good tent, one that stays dry inside even during a prolonged thunderstorm, is worth its weight in gold (and costs about as much). Even if it hasn't rained overnight, the rainfly of a tent is usually wet from dew and perspiration in the morning. Packing up a wet tent isn't fun. Pitching a tent in a downpour is worse. No matter how adept the camper, the interior will take on water.

Depending upon the terrain, tent sites may be plentiful or hard to come by. A one-person tent needs only a relatively level spot of two feet by seven feet. On a rocky trail, even such a modest wish may go unfulfilled. Here, then, is another reason why modern trail apps are so useful: They show campsites.

A favorite shelter of ultralight thru-hikers is the enclosed hammock. Its advantages? It's light and can be pitched anywhere—no need for cleared ground so long as there are two sturdy trees nearby.

TOP: Some thru-hikers prefer sheltering in hammocks, which need no cleared ground, only two adjacent trees.
BOTTOM: The author's tent rests on a natural bed of pine needles in Brush Mountain Wilderness.

Occasionally, every hiker needs a break from the daily grind, a vacation from the vacation, so to speak. At such times, a motel or hostel serves up just what the doctor ordered: a soft bed, a luxurious hot shower, and a high-calorie and/or home-cooked meal with a salad. For example, in Daleville, just where the AT crosses U.S. 220, there's a Super 8 Motel with an adjacent Pizza Hut. For a long-distance hiker, it doesn't get much better than that. I've stayed twice at the motel, once at the end of a section-hike when I was too weary and beat up from a fall to drive home and a second time in order to get an early morning jump on an 800-foot climb before ninety-degree summer heat kicked in.

There's no shortage of hostels in Virginia accessible to AT hikers. Their reputations vary. I figure these are usually for the younger crowd, so I generally bypass them. But I'd heard so much about Woods Hole Hostel on Pearis Mountain that I made a point to stay there on a section-hike in 2018. Woods Hole did not disappoint. It's a unique place, a bit of a Shangri-La, with a fascinating history to boot.

In 1939, Roy and Tillie Wood from Roswell, Georgia, discovered a rustic, chestnut-log cabin in Sugar Run Valley on Pearis Mountain and holed up for a year while Roy completed a master's thesis on elk populations in southwest Virginia. Over time, Roy and Tillie bought 100 acres and the cabin, renting it for forty years to hunters. In 1981, Roy retired from the Department of the Interior, and for the next five years he and Tillie lovingly restored "Woods Hole," often with a passel of grandkids in tow. In 1986, having added a chestnut-log bunkhouse to the property, they opened Woods Hole as a hostel for AT hikers. A year later, Roy died of heart failure, just after putting finishing touches on yet another renovation. Tillie continued to run Woods Hole Hostel for twenty-one years until she passed of cancer in 2007. Her dying concern: Who would continue the hostel?

Enter Neville, one of Roy and Tillie's grandchildren. Neville was a natural; after all, she'd visited her grandparents at Woods Hole since the age of four. In 2009, she and husband, Michael, moved there permanently from Georgia to continue the family hosteling tradition. The pair had met at Woods Hole in 2005, when Michael passed through while thru-hiking the AT.[3]

What they've since built together is remarkable. Woods Hole is an organic farm as well as a hostel. The main house now has two B&B rooms. Neville and Michael are both artsy, and artistic flourishes adorn every corner of Woods Hole. The bunkhouse is small but charming. The new bathhouse—its water heated by a wood furnace—is simultaneously functional, rustic, and tastefully decorated with knick-knacks and remnants of tile.

In the summer of 2018, Woods Hole added two screened safari tents on raised platforms, with lovely views of Sugar Run Valley. I rented one for a night of "glamping" (glamour camping) during a challenging section-hike. A few extra bucks buy a home-cooked organic dinner and/or breakfast. Hikers are expected to help in the kitchen or

The homey bunkhouse at Woods Hole Hostel (top), as seen from the main house, is small but inviting. The bunkhouse's interior (bottom) exudes rustic charm and is stocked with hiker amenities, including a refrigerator with cold soft drinks available on the honor system. Alcohol is not permitted at Woods Hole.

Woods Hole Hostel (top) is well worth the half-mile (.8-kilometer) detour downhill from the ridge of Pearis Mountain. The queen beds in the safari tents (bottom) near the hostel are luxurious after several nights of slumber on hard ground, and the views from the screened front door in good weather are superb.

At Woods Hole Hostel, hikers can indulge in "glamping" by renting a safari tent.

around the farm, which, in this hiker's estimation, only adds to the camaraderie and one's appreciation of the labor of love that is Woods Hole.

Another hostel with a great reputation is Bear Garden Hiker Hostel, just off VA 42 south of Ceres, Virginia. I stayed there in August 2019, the night before embarking on a daunting twenty-seven-mile section along Garden Mountain, my last remaining major section-hike to all but complete the AT in the Virginias. Bear Garden is a no-frills hostel, but it's well thought out, well stocked with hiker necessities, and situated just 100 yards or so off the trail.

Bear Garden Hiker Hostel (top) on VA 42 near Ceres, Virginia, is both spartan and welcoming. At the bunkhouse (below), hostel proprietors Bob and Bertie Lingham bookend "Boots" and his dog, Bella, soon to hit the trail following a respite. The hostel's other structures include a privy, shower, and chapel.

At Hickory Ridge Campground in Grayson Highlands State Park, seven-tenths of a mile (1.1 kilometers) from the AT via a blue-blazed spur trail, campers or hikers can rent yurts.

Best of all, proprietors Bob and Bertie Lingham are as gracious and accommodating as can be. Opened in 2017, Bear Garden is the fulfillment of retirement dreams. Bob, a retired middle-school science teacher, and Bertie, a retired ICU nurse, are from Michigan. For years they'd looked—in several states, with hosteling in mind—for property along the AT. Eventually, they found forty acres near Ceres. Several years and a lot of TLC later, Bear Garden beckons weary pilgrims, mends their ragged bodies and flagging spirits, and sends them on their way in far better shape than when they arrived.

An unusual lodging option can be found at Grayson Highlands State Park, which has recently erected four yurts on the fringes of its main campground. Each sits in the woods on a massive, raised deck. Amenities include a grill and deck chairs. A blue-blazed trail, seven-tenths of a mile long, leads from the AT to the camp store at the entrance to the campground.

Finally, if one wants luxury accommodations, those exist, too. Several historic lodges can be found in close proximity to the AT. Skyland and Big Meadows Waysides on the Skyline Drive, just ten miles apart, offer rustic lodges with restaurants. Each is literally a stone's throw from the trail. During the summer of 2015, I "slack-packed" two sections of the AT through Shenandoah National Park. (When slack-packing, one takes only a day

Relative to most accommodations near the AT, Peaks of Otter Lodge, shown here at dusk, is pure luxury. The lodge is closed during the winter, as is the restaurant overlooking Abbott Lake, named for Stanley William Abbott (1908–1975), the Blue Ridge Parkway's first resident landscape architect and planner.

pack and counts on civilized amenities for sustenance and lodging.) The second twenty-mile section began at Skyland and ended at the South River Picnic Area. I broke the trip midway at Big Meadows, where Suzanne and our daughter, Elena, met me at the lodge.

Farther south, just off the Blue Ridge Parkway and around three miles from the AT, Peaks of Otter Lodge lies in a jewel of a setting, nestled on a twenty-four-acre lake among three significant peaks: Sharp Top, Flat Top, and Harkening Hill. For three summers during my college years, I worked near there as a counselor at a primitive boys' camp, and I retain affection for Peaks of Otter and its environs. On my first section-hike south of the James River, I'd pre-arranged for Suzanne to meet me at a given time and milepost on the Parkway and then for us to explore my old stomping ground. We had a lovely experience during which, despite having hiked Sharp Top and Flat Top countless times, I claimed Harkening Hill for the very first time.

There may be trail purists for whom glamping is heretical. On the other hand, if one wishes to experience all the riches of the AT, natural and human-made, then sampling different types of shelter only heightens that experience.

TOP: At Mount Rogers National Recreation Area's Visitor Center, hikers can find snacks, flush toilets, and bus transportation into nearby Marion, Virginia, the county seat of Smyth County and a good place to resupply.

BOTTOM: Amenities are few and far between on the AT, but upscale B&Bs, eateries, ice-cream parlors, and other amenities lie just blocks from the trail as it winds through hilly, historic Harpers Ferry, West Virginia.

TOP: For AT hikers, Bears Den Hostel and Trail Center near VA 7 is a mecca beloved for its historic stone mansion, west-facing views, and many amenities, including Wi-Fi.

BOTTOM: Blackburn Trail Center was built in 1913 as a summer cottage by a D.C.-based physician and transformed during the 1980s into a trail-maintenance hub and hiker's way station by the Potomac Appalachian Trail Club (PATC).

Even today, the interior of Blackburn Trail Center (top) provides the rustic ambience of the original mountain cabin. Above the mantel at Blackburn Trail Center, a plaque (below) commemorates benefactors Fred and Ruth Blackburn, who helped transform a ramshackle woodland cabin near Round Hill, Virginia, into the current beehive of trail maintenance. In 2019, Round Hill was designated an Appalachian Trail Community by the ATC.

TOP: Damascus, Virginia, on U.S. 58 has long been a quintessential trail town. Here, the AT and Virginia Creeper Trail, a multi-purpose rail-to-trail path, converge. A mecca for outdoor recreation enthusiasts of many stripes, Damascus has the feel of a mini Moab, Utah, with lots of outdoor outfitters and eateries. The town historically swells to overflowing once a year, during the Appalachian Trail Days event in May, billed, according to organizers, as the "the largest A.T.-specific celebration in the world." Regrettably, on September 28, 2024, Hurricane Helene and its twenty inches (50.8 centimeters) of rain had a "devastating impact" on Damascus, with downtown suffering significant flooding from Laurel Creek. The road to recovery may be long, but it is well underway.[4]

BOTTOM: This fading mural on an abandoned building alongside the Virginia Creeper Trail depicts "Moonlight Over Damascus."

"Trail towns" offer up a hiker's hat-trick: shelter or lodging, resupply opportunities, and eateries. The section of trail in the Virginias that I completed is bookended by two quintessential trail towns: Damascus, on the Virginia/Tennessee border to the south, and Harpers Ferry, on the West Virginia/Maryland border, to the north (see pages 6 and 76). In between are sixteen additional official Appalachian Trail Communities or "trail towns" for short (from southwest to northeast Virginia): Abingdon, Damascus, Marion/Smyth County, Bland County, Narrows, Pearisburg, Troutville, Glasgow, Buena Vista, Nelson County, Waynesboro, Harrisonburg, Elkton, Luray/Page County, Front Royal/Warren County, Berryville/Clarke County, Round Hill. In West Virginia, Harpers Ferry and nearby Bolivar join to form that trail community.

Damascus, Pearisburg, and Harpers Ferry lie directly on the AT, and the AT traverses Main Street in Damascus for the better part of a mile. Most trail towns, however, are too far off trail for a hiking detour, so these communities rely on several options: trail-angel drivers, paid shuttle services, or bus service. Marion, for example, runs a shuttle bus several times daily to ferry hikers between the town and Mount Rogers National Recreation Area's Visitor Center (see page 115, top) about ten miles to the east of Marion and adjacent to Partnership Shelter (see page 104, top).

Lodging in trail towns can run the gambit from campgrounds to cabins, to hostels, to B&Bs, to rustic inns and hotels, even to spas like The Martha (previously known as the Martha Washington Inn) in Abingdon. Two trail towns—Damascus and Waynesboro—currently provide free camping in municipal campgrounds, with potable water and toilets. Trail-town eateries also range widely: from diners to hamburger, barbeque, or pizza joints; from all-you-can-eat buffets to upscale restaurants. Other trail-town amenities include laundromats, outfitters, post offices, banks and ATM machines, grocery stores, creameries, breweries, and coffee shops with Wi-Fi.

Trail towns embody reciprocity. Local activists and trail angels organize to formalize a community's care for nearby sections of the AT and for the needs of the hikers who walk them. In return, hikers contribute to the local economy, and easy trail access contributes to the health of the community. As a fitting symbol of this symbiosis, the Explore More Discovery Museum, Harrisonburg's children's museum, features an Appalachian Trail exhibit. That trail towns keep popping up more than a century after Benton MacKaye first floated his idea for "An Appalachian Trail" is testament to the inspiration and robustness of that vision.

Stony Man Summit (maximum elevation 4,011 feet/1,223 meters) in Shenandoah National Park, a favorite of day-hikers, is accessed by either an AT spur trail or from Skyline Drive, visible in the distance. Photograph by Suzanne Fiederlein and used by permission.

EIGHT

Spurs

Two roads diverged in a wood, and I—
I took the one less traveled by,
And that has made all the difference.[1]

—ROBERT FROST

SIDE TRAILS THAT BRANCH DIRECTLY off the AT are known as "spur trails." Marked with the same single- and double-blaze conventions as the AT, spur trails are blazed in blue paint that ranges from robin-egg to royal blue in hue. Other trails in the vicinity of the AT, but not direct spurs, are blazed typically in yellow, red, or orange.

As often as not, AT shelters lie a tenth of a mile or more off the main trail. Spur trails take the weary hiker there. North of the James River, Virginia's semi-isolated shelters include David Lesser Memorial Shelter, Whiskey Hollow Shelter, Gravel Springs Hut, Pass Mountain Hut, Bearfence Mountain Hut, Hightop Hut, Blackrock Hut, Calf Mountain Shelter, Punchbowl Shelter, and Cow Camp Gap Shelter. For reasons unbeknownst to the author, most shelters in Shenandoah National Park are termed "huts." In the category of remoteness, Cow Camp Gap Shelter takes the cake. It lies on a fire road six-tenths of a mile off the AT. South of the James, access to Helveys Mill, Saunders, Hurricane Mountain, or Trimpi Shelters requires a bit of extra mileage amongst blue blazes.

As mentioned in *Chapter Four: Water*, shelters are normally co-located with water sources. Still, the source may lie a few tenths of a mile from the shelter. In such cases, blue blazes may lead the thirsty hiker to a spring or creek. In the category of water inconvenience, the David Lesser Memorial Shelter is notable. It's a quarter-mile down a steep, switchbacked grade to the shelter's spring.

Spur trails also lead to water sources near but not on the AT. Never have I been so relieved to see blue blazes leading to a reliable spring than on Pearis Mountain. I'd hiked south from Woods Hole Hostel for nine and one-half miles on the mountain's nearly waterless ridge and was seriously low on water. Just before the 2,000-foot plunge into Pearisburg, which I intended to save for the next day, a well-marked spur trail on the left

Spur trails, like Trail Boss Trail near Bastian, Virginia, are blazed with blue paint. Trails that are directly connected to the AT are marked in blue, whereas those not directly connected to the AT are marked in yellow, red, and orange.

led across a mountaintop flat to an oasis: a piped spring and campsites for half a dozen tents. It was a perfect spot to end a near-perfect day.

The AT hits most of the highlights along its right-of-way. But not all. Spur trails take the curious hiker to natural gems worthy of extra exertion. In Shenandoah National Park, spurs lead to Mary's Rock, Stony Man, Calvary Rocks, and Glass Hollow overlooks as well as to Lewis Spring and South River Falls. South of Pearisburg along Dismal Creek, a side trail leads to Dismal Falls. Farther south, near Bastian, Virginia, the AT skirts along the southern rim of Burke's Garden, an upland, bowl-shaped valley eight miles long by four miles wide. The half-mile Davis Farm spur trail leads steeply down from the ridge to a campsite at an old homestead. Another tenth of a mile farther, there's an intermittent spring. Still further south, near Grayson Highlands State Park, a spur leads to the summit of Mount Rogers (elevation 5,729 feet), Virginia's highest point. And from the camp store at Grayson's Hickory Ridge Campground, the red-blazed Wilson Creek Trail skirts for

To access Wilson Creek Trail in Grayson Highlands State Park, follow the blue blazes from the AT to Hickory Ridge Campground, then follow the red blazes along the headwaters of impressive Wilson Creek. Wilson Creek eventually flows into the New River—incongruously, one of the oldest rivers in the world—near appropriately named Mouth-of-Wilson, Virginia.

Multiple spur trails converge at mile-high Rhododendron Gap (elevation 5,350 feet/1,631 meters), a high-country crossroads in Mount Rogers National Recreation Area. Among these are Rhododendron Gap Trail, Crest Trail, and Wilburn Ridge Trail.

a mile along tumultuous Wilson Creek, as it drops precipitously from its high headwaters. Spurs lead to welcome respites as well: to hostels such as Four Pines, Bears Den and Woods Hole or into resupply towns like Catawba.

By combining spur trails with sections of the AT, one can create some memorable loop hikes. In Shenandoah National Park, for example, Mary's Run spur, Riprap spur, and a 3.5-mile section of the AT create a triangular loop trail eleven miles in length and featuring the Calvary Rocks overlook and a swimming hole along Riprap Creek. A bit farther south and half as long, the Big Run Loop Trail combines with the AT to form a six-mile circuit. Those who prefer a short rock scramble can combine the Bearfence Rock Scramble Loop Trail with the AT for a two-mile circuit. And, along the Blue Ridge Parkway, the three-mile Mau-Har Trail bypasses the AT's assault of Three Ridges. Combining the AT and the alternate route creates a strenuous six-mile loop.

Still further south, other loops combine the AT with Dragons Tooth Trail, Ribble Trail, Trail Boss Trail, or Pine Mountain Trail. The latter of these is spectacular. Near Mount Rogers, the AT takes a massive U-shaped bend to the south, presumably to offer

Near Rhododendron Gap in Mount Rogers National Recreation Area, the AT and the blue-blazed Wilburn Ridge Trail run parallel, affording day-hikers a circuit-hike option.

hikers the amenities of Grayson Highlands State Park as well as the magnificent vistas of Grayson's upland balds. Pine Mountain Trail short-circuits the U by cutting across its top. The spur, which originates to the south at Rhododendron Gap, is itself breathtaking. Combining the two trails turns the U into an O and affords a circuit hike without peer.

The 200,000-acre Mount Rogers National Recreation Area, by the way, has something for everyone: hiking, camping, horseback-riding, bicycling, trout-fishing, picnicking, and cross-country skiing. In addition to 500 miles of trails, including sixty miles of the AT, the recreation area has eleven U.S. Forest Service campgrounds, four of which are designated for horseback riders along the sixty-seven-mile Virginia Highlands Horse Trail. The recreation area is also home to four designated national wilderness areas: Lewis Fork, Little Wilson Creek, Raccoon Branch, and Little Dry Run Wildernesses.

The Mount Rogers National Recreation Area also features the thirty-three-mile multi-purpose Virginia Creeper Trail, which connects the "trail towns" of Abington and Damascus, Virginia. The Creeper Trail is a rail-to-recreation trail for biking, jogging, and walking. It features forty-seven wooden trestles. One terminus is Whitetop Station, at

North of Mountain Lake Wilderness, a short spur trail leads to Kelly Knob, a favorite destination for day-hikers and a recommended detour for all others, with imposing rocks, winsome views, and radiant wild azaleas and mountain laurel blooming in May and June. (Also, see page 144.)

Three international friends (left to right: Vera from Berlin, Germany, Khalid from Egypt, and Courtney from the U.S.) enjoy a fall lunch and companionship at Spy Rock on a brisk October day in 2022. The trio met while studying graduate economics in Berlin. On a short spur trail a few miles/kilometers south of The Priest (elevation 4,063 feet/1,238 meters), Spy Rock is a popular day-hike destination in Nelson County, Virginia, with unencumbered 360-degree views.

3,500-feet elevation on the flank of Whitetop Mountain (elevation 5,520 feet), Virginia's second-highest peak. Numerous outfitters in Abingtom and Damascus provide bicycle rentals and shuttle services. From Whitetop Station it's a seventeen-mile run to Damascus, all downhill. Along the way, bicyclists will meet AT hikers at several junctures of the two iconic trails, which combine briefly in Damascus.

Mount Rogers and its eponymous national recreation area are named after William Barton Rogers (1804–1882), Virginia's first state geologist. After teaching "natural philosophy" at the College of William and Mary and the University of Virginia, Barton moved to Massachusetts to found the Massachusetts Institute of Technology (M.I.T.) in 1861.

One of my all-time favorite blue-blaze experiences involves the AT at Cole Mountain. The area lies deep in the George Washington National Forest in high country north of

TOP: There are no visible indications of human habitation in this vast view to the south from the western peak of twin-peaked Mount Pleasant, accessed from the Henry Lanum Loop Trail.
BOTTOM: Near remote Hog Camp on the AT, two circuit trails connect to form a twelve-mile (19.3-kilometer) figure eight of unusual scenic variety. One loop, the Henry Lanum Loop Trail, ascends to Mount Pleasant (elevation 4,071 feet/1,241 meters), as shown above.

U.S. 60 and east of the Blue Ridge Parkway. Two six-mile circuit hikes originate at remote Hog Camp Gap in Amherst County: the Cole Mountain Loop and the Mount Pleasant Loop. The former incorporates a three-mile section of the AT, which passes through the highland meadows of Cole Mountain, and the Hotel Trail, a spur on which the Cow Camp Gap Shelter is located. The latter reaches Mount Pleasant via the Henry Lanum Loop Trail, which combines a footpath and a mountain-laurel-endowed fire road to form a loop. Combining the two loops creates a twelve-mile figure-eight hike, with two small parking areas located at the nexus of the eight. A second spur trail, eight-tenths of a mile in length—a spur on a spur—summits Mount Pleasant from the Lanum Trail. Mount Pleasant features twin peaks, each with a commanding view. The west-facing peak offers a rock outcrop with an unobstructed westward view of undulating mountains, including Cole Mountain, with no visible sign of human presence. Between the two peaks several small, grass-covered campsites lie nestled among comely rock formations. At the base of the peaks on another short spur lies a small spring.

Four times now, I have traveled in this backcountry, twice on day-hikes with friends on the Henry Lanum Loop Trail and twice while backpacking, once with friends and once solo. Rain hampered both backpacking trips. Thus, Cole Mountain remains on my bucket list. I've yet to see the views that everyone raves about. Look out Cole Mountain, here I come, once again.

Early-morning rays pierce the mixed-hardwood forest along the AT on Pearis Mountain (highest elevation 3,770 feet/1,149 meters) in Giles County, Virginia. The land here is part of the expansive 1.8-million-acre (784,434-hectare) George Washington-Jefferson National Forest, one of the largest areas of public land in the Eastern United States that extends beyond Virginia and West Virginia into eastern Kentucky. Its drainage basin includes the New, Kanawha, Ohio, and Mississippi Rivers. Rain here thus flows into either the Atlantic Ocean or the Gulf of Mexico.

NINE

Flora

One thing I have learned in the woods
is that there is no such thing as random.
Everything is steeped in meaning, colored
by relationship, one thing with another.[1]

—ROBIN WALL KIMMERER

THE APPALACHIAN MOUNTAINS abound in biodiversity. Here reside more plant and animal species than in any other temperate forest on the planet. In Appalachian field and forest, species of flora alone number more than 2,000.[2]

Among the hardwoods native to the uplands of Appalachia are more than a dozen species of oaks; maples of numerous varieties, including red, sugar, and silver maple; hickories, principally bitternut and shagbark; ash; beech; birch; chestnut; tulip poplar; elm; black locust; hornbeam; redbud; dogwood; magnolia; sassafras; sweetgum; black gum; holly; cherry; walnut; sycamore; mulberry; willow; and more.

Each majestic species has a story to tell. None is more compelling than that of the American chestnut (*Castanea dentata*), which thrived for forty million years, only to succumb, a century past, to a fungal blight. Four human generations ago, an estimated four billion chestnuts—among the largest, most stately, and fastest-growing of hardwoods—dominated Eastern forests. Pioneers prized chestnut wood, straight-grained and decay-resistant, for multiple uses: split-rail fencing, furniture, building material, and, later, for railroad ties.[3] Bountiful chestnut mast fed forest creatures, hogs, and humans, the latter especially during the holiday season of "Chestnuts roasting on an open fire . . ." By the 1930s, the chestnut blight had felled nearly all, the greatest forest disaster in recorded history.

As mentioned previously in *Chapter 7: Shelter*, during my college years I worked at a primitive summer camp near Peaks of Otter on the Blue Ridge Parkway. Counselors and campers lived in tents, cooked three meals daily on open fires, and took cold showers. Most of the firewood we gathered was fallen chestnut, which had not rotted in the decades since the blight. The wood is unique. Straight-grained and soft, it splits like pine yet

Thickets of purple rhododendron (*Rhododendron catawbiense*), interspersed among oak, hickory, and other hardwoods, contrast and grace the AT with vibrant color.

produces coals like hardwood. (At the other extreme is black locust, which refuses to split because of its twisted grain, and produces an oily, acrid smoke when burning.)

The poet Henry Wordsworth Longfellow (1807–1882) immortalized the chestnut, integral to American life, in the opening lines of his poem, "The Village Blacksmith" (1840): "Under the spreading chestnut tree,/The village smithy stands . . ."[4] Why then is chestnut, now long gone, still listed as an Appalachian hardwood? In a fluke of nature, the blight does not kill the roots, and chestnuts continue to send up shoots. Chestnut sprouts abound along the AT. They reach adolescence, then die. The hope is that natural selection or genetic engineering will produce a blight-resistant chestnut before the iconic tree is fully extinct.

Unfortunately, many of America's iconic trees are now in trouble of one kind or another. Conifers also grace the Appalachians and its namesake trail, particularly at higher elevations: at least a half-dozen varieties of pines, including white and Virginia pine, as well as spruce, hemlock, and cedar. Eastern or Canadian hemlock (*Tsuga canadensis*), shade-tolerant but thirsty, used to thrive on the flanks of creeks.

TOP: Sassafras seedlings (*Sassafras albidum*), distinctive for three types of leaves—left-handed, right-handed, and thumbless mittens—contribute to ground cover to the right of the AT. Sassafras roots are the principal flavoring in root beer, which used to be known as sarsaparilla.
BOTTOM: Down but not out. Despite being decimated during the early 1900s by a fungal blight, the once-dominant American chestnut (*Castanea dentata*) survives along the AT as small shoots recognizable by distinctive serrated leaves.

Even death can be beautiful on the AT. Here, a colorful mold, most likely raspberry slime mold (*Tubifera ferruginosa*), slowly reclaims a rotting log.

Hemlocks, unlike the chestnut, have been savaged by a tiny pest, in this case an aphid-like insect known as the Hemlock woolly adelgid (*Adelges tsugae*). Adelgids slipped into North America by accident, on imported Asian hemlock, which is naturally resistant to the pest. Adelgids suck the sap of the hemlock, and the trees die of malnutrition. Climate change may have exacerbated the hemlock's demise, because winters are no longer cold enough to kill off the adelgid in sufficient numbers. In Virginia, one now finds very sick hemlocks or hemlock skeletons.

Another invasive pest, this one from the Far East, the emerald ash borer (*Agrilus planipennis*), is now decimating the White ash, or American ash (*Fraxinus america*). Pandemics don't just affect humans. For decades many our trees have been fighting for their lives, as documented by Charles Little in his book *The Dying of the Trees: The Pandemic in America's Trees* (1995). Little's book has done for forests what Rachel Carson's *Silent Spring* did for birds. In almost every case, we humans find ourselves culpable, either by our transport of invasives or our impact on Earth's climate.

Careful what you say while hiking at Kelly Knob: This magical, gnarled oak tree appears to have ears! (Also, see pages 96 and 98.)

When walking the AT, one's eyes are most often cast downward, riveted on the trail itself. It's a hiker's habit formed to minimize tripping on rocks or slipping on wet roots. The hiker therefore becomes well acquainted with ground-level flora. The forest floor along the Virginia AT is mostly a profusion of varieties of bushes and ground cover, some flowering, some not. But occasionally one stumbles onto a ground-cover monoculture. These vary from place to place, elevation to elevation, soil type to soil type. Most common at high elevations is the ferned forest floor, but, here and there, one will find acres almost exclusively of jewelweed or immense patches of mayapple or nettles. Go figure. I hike in shorts, so my least-favorite ground cover is the stinging nettle. Through many unwelcome encounters with these prickly plants, I've learned a little trick: After the sting comes the itch. Don't scratch the itch, and discomfort soon passes.

TOP: Near Buchanan, Virginia, the AT threads through the George Washington National Forest, here carpeted in jewelweed (*Impatiens capensis*), also known as spotted touch-me-not, common in moist, shaded areas. It blooms from June until the first frost, usually in early October. Juice from the leaves and stems of jewelweed was used as a traditional Native American folk remedy for skin rashes, including poison ivy.
BOTTOM: This verdant ridgetop is two miles (3.2 kilometers) south of Mount Rogers National Recreation Area's Visitor Center.

TOP: Ground cover along the AT varies dramatically with elevation, moisture, and soil type. At higher reaches, ferns, such as the eastern hay-scented fern (*Dennstaedtia punctilobula*) shown here, are common.
BOTTOM: Thickets of ferns along the AT always create a sense of a primeval world, in which nature is both sublime and supreme.

On the AT, the ordinary often turns extraordinary. Here, boulders blend in among ferns and wildflowers at the southern edge of Loft Mountain Campground and its 207 sites.

On a brighter note, in spring and summer the forest floor through which the AT winds erupts in a riot of color. Keeping track of this abundance of wildflowers requires a far better taxonomist than I, but here are a few flowering plants that I learned to recognize and appreciate years ago, while a camp counselor: fire pink, Deptford pink, American columbine, trillium, jewelweed (also known as spotted-touch-me-not), mayapple, and blood root (*Sanguinaria canadensis*). The rhizome of blood root has orange flesh with red-orange sap. On the first day of a fresh camp week, we'd ritually sacrifice one blood root plant to brand our new campers as blood brothers, a practice now ill-advised by the hiker's maxim: "Take nothing but photos; leave nothing but footprints."

Later in the summer, blackberries and raspberries ripen at sunny spots along the trail. These are usually picked over by other hikers and certainly by bears. And in the higher elevations, such as Grayson Highlands, huckleberries—a type of small, wild blueberry—thrive. Fresh fruit, especially that which need not be carried, is a boon to any long-distance hiker.

The principal pollinator of fire pink (*Silene virginica*), common on the AT's rocky slopes, is the ruby-throated hummingbird (*Archilochus colubris*). To accommodate the hummingbird's migration from Central America and Mexico to Canada, fire pink blooms from April through August.

A friendly fern nestles against a stately toadstool—likely a common mushroom (*Leucoagaricus leucothites*). The "shrooms" grow in late summer through fall but occasionally appear in spring.

ABOVE: White trillium (*Trillium grandiflorum*) is another common trailside delight in the Virginias that hikers never tire of seeing. It usually blooms in late March and early April.

OPPOSITE TOP: Mayapple (*Podophyllum peltatum*) predominates the ground cover on this sunny and relatively flat ridge. Mayapple blooms often emerge in April.

OPPOSITE BOTTOM: Pink lady's slipper or moccasin flower (*Cypripedium acaule*), a variety of wild orchid, is virtually impossible to cultivate because of its dependence on forest fungi, yet it grows naturally along the AT in spring. Delicate but seductive, lady's slipper entraps pollinating bumble bees via a one-way entrance. The only exit is through a snug passage that contains the flower's reproductive parts. These lady's slippers are huddled on a rocky ridge just south of Dragons Tooth (see page 60).

TOP: Vegetation along the AT varies dramatically with elevation. Mosses, ferns, and lichen, shown here, are typical of high country.

BOTTOM: Delicate saxifrages (*Micranthes caroliniana*), common to Alaska and alpine meadows, can also be found in the high country of Mount Rogers National Recreation Area. Here, a saxifrage snuggles against rocks on Wilburn Ridge. It blooms in April and May.

TOP: It's a hiker's rare thrill to stumble upon the vibrancy of eastern red columbine (*Aquilegia canadensis*), prized by Native Americans for its medicinal properties and by the Royal Horticultural Society for its brilliance. It blooms from April to July. **BOTTOM**: A trailside profusion of ground cover includes common buttercups (*Ranunculus acris*), which blooms in April and May.

In addition to offering stunning views and unusual rock formations, the spur trail to Kelly Knob delights with flowering vegetation, including (top) mountain laurel (*Kalmia latifolia*) and (bottom) flame azaleas (*Rhododendron calendulaceum*) in flaming orange. (Also, see pages 96, 98, and 126.)

A rare mountain azalea (*Rhododendron prinophyllum*), in its full pink glory usually blooms in June and early July.

Mountain laurel, rhododendron, and azaleas are closely related flowering shrubs of the heather, or *Ericaceae*, family. The first two occur in great abundance along the trail in the Virginias. Indeed, the great laurel (*Rhododendron maximum*) is the state flower of West Virginia. Whereas rhododendron most often flourish along the banks of streams, laurel prefer rocky trails. Both are beautiful in bloom. Wild azaleas are rarer. I've encountered only a few: two with flaming-orange blossoms, another in pink. The first orange one made such an impression that I recall exactly where I was at the moment: Kelly Knob.

Indian pipe (*Monotropa uniflora*) bursts forth in the Appalachian highlands when saturating rains follow a dry spell. Known also as the ghost plant, Indian pipe lives parasitically, its waxy white stems and leaves containing no chlorophyll. It flowers from early summer to early autumn.

When I close my eyes to reflect on the most vivid images that countless hours of hiking Virginia's AT have burned into my consciousness, there I see mountain laurel and rhododendron in all their arboreal splendor. When such glory peaks depends upon time of year and elevation. Mountain laurel blooms in mid-spring at the lower elevations along the AT, progressing up the mountainsides as spring matures. So, too, for rhododendron. Thus, at the right elevation, one can catch either or both in bloom throughout the spring and early summer. June is usually a reliable time to see both.

Woods dark and deep, lichen-encrusted boulders watched over by vigilant laurel, ferned forest floors, rhododendron tunnels, flaming wildflowers: indelible images for any hiker attentive to the floral extravagance of the AT in the Virginias.

TOP: Siebold's arrowwood (*Vibernum sieboldii*) is an invasive plant that occurs in Virginia in a few isolated spots, including here on the Loft Mountain Wayside spur trail. The fruit clusters from early to late fall. Invasive species are a constant management issue along the AT. **BOTTOM**: Woodland sunflowers (*Helianthus divericatus*) brighten the AT from July to September.

Along the AT, white-tailed deer, also known as Virginia deer (*Odocoileus virginianus*), are common though skittish. They are often seen in the early morning and early evening foraging in meadows and along forest edges. Photograph by Karen Atwood (© AtwoodPhoto/Karen E. H. Atwood) and used by permission.

TEN

Wildlife

The time will soon be here when my grandchild will long for the cry of a loon, the flash of a salmon, the whisper of spruce needles, or the screech of an eagle.[1]

—CHIEF DAN GEORGE

In one regard, the AT of the Virginias has caught me by complete surprise: I've actually seen precious little wildlife while hiking all these years. On second thought, it's not so surprising. One is more likely to see wildlife that is habituated to human life. Much of the AT in the Virginias passes through remote country: national forests and designated wilderness areas. The critters here—at least in areas away from visitor centers and campgrounds—are wild and not habituated. I've seen far more squirrels and rabbits in the yards of my Harrisonburg neighborhood than on the AT. In fact, I don't recall ever seeing a rabbit while hiking. Chipmunks, yes, and I recently saw one blissfully devouring a toadstool whole. Squirrels, yes but rarely.

On the other hand, deer are common, though skittish. A few summers ago, I learned something about deer I didn't know—and nearly jumped out of my skin. I was hiking alone on an AT section between Peaks of Otter and Daleville. The woods were quiet, and the trail was rutted but level, with considerable brush to each side. Just as I passed by a nondescript spot, a deafening "bleat" erupted from the brush on my left. Despite carrying a thirty-pound pack, I leapt a couple of feet into the air, or so it seemed at the time. The culprit: a fawn separated from its mama. I hadn't known beforehand that fawns bleat or that that is how a doe locates her prodigal offspring. A half-hour later, a couple of faster SOBOs overtook me. The fawn had bleated at them also, but they happily reported that doe and fawn were now reunited. My only other encounter with a fawn occurred years ago, while day-hiking the massive meadow at Big Meadows Wayside along the Skyline Drive in Shenandoah National Park. Far from the road, at a grassy depression near the base of a large rock, my wife, Suzanne, and I stumbled upon a blissfully sleeping fawn. We relished the picture of tranquility for a long time; the fawn never awakened.

American black bears (*Ursus americanus*) are plentiful on the AT, especially in Great Smoky Mountains National Park and Shenandoah National Park (SNP). I've twice encountered them at Matthews Arm Campground at mile 22.1 of the Skyline Drive. Campgrounds in both parks have bear vaults for food storage, and trail shelters within SNP provide bear poles. Most bears are not problematic, but rogue or "nuisance" bears—ones that have become acclimated to humans and human food and have thus lost the instinct to fear humans—can be unpredictable and dangerous.

Three summers ago, two friends and I hiked a section of the AT at the tail end of SNP. There was little water to be had along that section, so we stashed two one-gallon jugs at the midpoint, where we intended to camp on the second night out, around 100 yards off the Skyline Drive. On day two, after hiking for hours in a steady rain, we approached our designated campsite with weary relief. On a tree just at the intersection of the AT and the short spur trail to our campsite was posted a warning about a nuisance bear in the immediate vicinity. Two minutes later, we found the campsite and set up tents in the rain. As my companions—wet and chilled to the bone—crawled into warm sleeping bags, I, snug in better raingear, went in search of the stashed water jugs. I found them. One was intact, the other empty, crushed and full of holes made by a bear's large claws.

A hiker also hopes to avoid encounters with venomous snakes—timber rattlers (*Crotalus horridus*) and copperheads (*Agkistrodon contortrix*)—relatively plentiful in the mountains of Virginia and West Virginia. Knock on wood, I've not run across any on my recent treks. I have, however, had a number of close calls over the years on day-hikes, especially during the summers when I worked as a camp counselor near Peaks of Otter. With fifty to sixty boys living all summer in the woods, close encounters with reptiles were inevitable. Each summer produced another snake story, including some squeakers, like this one.

We lived in canvas wall tents, set up on wooden platforms, two campers on cots to a tent. Counselors lived alone, also in large wall tents, with the amenities of a mattressed bed and a footlocker full of all one's worldly possessions. One evening late, our camp's business manager, lying on his bed, decided he needed a caloric nightcap before turning off the trusty Coleman lantern. He reached for a bag of peanuts in his open footlocker, when something caught his eye. Good thing. A small timber rattler had beaten him to the peanuts.

And then there was my most unnerving experience. Every Tuesday at the camp, we spent the better part of the day hiking either Sharp Top or Flat Top at Peaks of Otter, an eight-mile round trip for the former and ten for the latter. This particular morning was glorious, with sun streaming through the forest canopy as we trod the trail from camp to the store at the base of Sharp Top. I led the group, with seven campers in the middle and my assistant counselor bringing up the rear. Right beside the trail was a bare, sunlit spot, which eight of us had passed when Jeff, my assistant, called out: "Dave, there's the biggest

A young bruin (top) at home among the ferns and an adult (bottom) roaming the forest. Although American black bears (*Ursus americanus*) thrive in their native habitat along the AT, seeing one is another matter. So it is always a thrill when a hiker encounters a bear in the wild, though one must always maintain a respectful distance. Photographs by Cindy Robinson and used by permission.

This male scarlet tanager (*Piranga olivacea*) is similar to the one seen by the author on an April hike on Brushy Mountain. Photograph by Karen Atwood (© AtwoodPhoto/Karen E. H. Atwood) and used by permission.

snake here I've ever seen!" I doubled back, and there, on the dirt patch alongside our path, was a timber rattler (*Crotalus horridus*), five feet in length and thicker than my upper arm. Mercifully, it was uncoiled and unfazed, happily basking in the sun. The guardian angels of young boys work overtime.

Given hazards like the slithery ones just mentioned and the predominance of rocky, uneven trail, a hiker's attention is most often focused downward, a few feet ahead. That's a bit of a shame, for the AT is a birder's paradise. Two springs ago, I saw my first scarlet tanager (*Piranga olivacea*), an unexpected thrill. If only I knew birds and bird calls better. Songbird symphonies in the early mornings are exquisitely delightful, but I never know who's singing which part.

The AT harbors fowl as well as songbirds. Occasionally, one runs across two or three wild turkeys (*Meleagris gallopavo*). If it had been up to Ben Franklin (1706–1790), we are told in American grade school, the wild turkey and not the bald eagle would have been America's national symbol: brains over brawn.[2] Then there are the amazing ruffled grouse (*Bonasa umbellus*). It's not uncommon to startle a grouse, and one's heart quickens when the bird beats its wings for flight, rustling dry leaves and piercing the stillness with a racket.

While hiking Rhododendron Gap Trail in Mount Rogers National Recreation Area, one might stumble upon misplaced Texas longhorns. Not exactly the wildlife one expects to see, but the AT does venture at times into the everyday agricultural landscape. (Also, see page 125.)

Speaking of unexpected encounters with animal life, I was once hiking near Rhododendron Gap on the Pine Mountain Trail that short-circuits the AT in the high country above Grayson Highlands State Park. Thickets of rhododendron stand on each side of the rocky and deeply rutted trail. One hikes in a miniature canyon. Ahead and on my right, I heard a monstrous thrashing amongst the rhododendron, and the beast appeared to be on a collision course with me. It must be a bear I thought, and there was nowhere to escape. When the creature bounded across the trail about twenty feet in front of me, I had to laugh. No bear, only a cow. How a cow wedged itself through that dense thicket was a wonder. It occurred to me almost instantaneously that deer and cows are both ruminants and must be related. So a cow, then, is a kind of domesticated deer. What else could explain a cow so at home in that brush?

In addition to its rogue cows, Grayson Highlands features a herd of wild ponies. They like handouts from AT hikers, a practice officially discouraged. And although it hasn't happened to me, grimy thru-hikers report having the salt licked off their legs by the friendly beasts. And twice when I was in wilderness, once on the AT and once in Laurel Fork

Near Massie's Gap along the AT in Grayson Highlands State Park, wild ponies graze. These few are among a herd of 150 whose foraging maintains the upland balds near Virginia's highest point, Mount Rogers (elevation 5,729 feet/1,746 meters). Photographs by Justin Hawkins (trail name "Sunrise Chaser") during his thru-hike in 2016, and used by permission.

Only by fortuitous happenstance did the author spot this common snapping turtle (*Chelydra serpentina*), semi-submerged in a wetland beside a boardwalk on the AT north of Marion, Virginia.

Wilderness, I've had eerie experiences that left me completely unnerved. Both times I was awakened from sound sleep in the wee hours of morning by the yelping of a pack of dogs or coyotes, I know not which. I would have been no match for either.

When I was a child, I frequently encountered common box turtles (*Terrapene carolina*) in the West Virginia woods. Alas, I can't remember the last time I ran across one in the wild, certainly not on any of my section-hikes along the AT. I did recently meet a snapping turtle (*Chelydra serpentina*), a complete surprise. Just north of its intersection with Interstate 81 near Groseclose, Virginia, the AT runs along a boardwalk through a small wetland area. What made me do it I don't know, but I stopped to glance in the water, and there, right where I paused, semi-submerged and camouflaged by flower petals, was a large snapper.

The AT's American green tree frogs (*Dryophytes cinereus*) must number in the billions. Their nightly serenades begin at dusk and wane just before daybreak, warmup acts for the songbirds. Though they are everywhere, I've yet to see one.

TOP: Were it not for a hop, this little fellow—most likely a common Fowler's toad (*Anaxyrus fowleri*) nearly obscured by ground cover—would have escaped detection. **BOTTOM**: A pair of snails inhabits an upended log with an impressive toadstool growing in its core on Harkening Hill Trail at Peaks of Otter. Photograph by Suzanne Fiederlein and used by permission.

A red eft, the terrestrial stage of the red-spotted or Eastern newt (*Notophthalmus viridescens*), is ubiquitous on Virginia's moist trails at high elevations and stands out starkly against the normal earth tones. The adult newt is surprisingly different than the fragile eft. The dark-green adult is aquatic, grows as long as five inches (12.7 centimeters), and lives for twelve to fifteen years.

Other than birds and occasional deer, the most ubiquitous creatures on the AT are millipedes—often crushed by a hiker's foot—toads, and newts. If it were up to me to pick a totem animal for the AT in the Virginias, it would be the red-spotted (or Eastern) newt (*Notophthalmus viridescens*), called a red eft during its delicate juvenile stage. These tiny fellows are common in mountainous Virginia, especially after rains. They're so delicate, so colorful.

On the subject of the AT's small creatures, let's give a shout out to pollinators. In addition to birds and bats, insects are prime pollinators: bees, butterflies, and beetles, among them. Pollinators have a symbiotic relationship with flowering plants. Flowers provide energy in the form of nectar and pollen. In return pollinators consummate the sexual act for flowers by transferring grains of pollen from the flower's male anatomy to its female part.

We humans may have flowers and pollinators to thank for our evolutionary emergence. Big-brained mammals sit high on the food chain, because large brains consume prodigious quantities of energy. The fruit of flowering plants is a concentrated source of energy not only for us, but also for the creatures lower on the food chain on which we depend for sustenance. It's estimated that seventy-five to ninety-five percent of all flowering plants depend on pollinators for fertilization. As a result, about one in every three bites of food we consume is thanks to a pollinator.[3]

TOP: The butterfly garden at the Harry F. Byrd Sr. Visitor Center at Big Meadows Wayside in Shenandoah National Park recreates a meadow habitat attractive to monarch butterflies (*Danaus lexippus*) and other insects, birds, and wildlife. Of the meadows on or near the AT in Virginia, Big Meadows on the Skyline Drive is managed by periodic controlled burns; in contrast, forest re-growth in Grayson Highlands is prevented by a herd of grazing ponies (see page 154).

BOTTOM: A ravenous monarch caterpillar (*Danaus plexippus*) feeds on a milkweed (*Asclepias*) leaf at the Big Meadows butterfly garden, delighting visitors—young and old—and AT hikers.

Southbound from Chestnut Knob (elevation 4,409 feet/1,344-kilometers) on Garden Mountain, the AT runs downhill for two miles (3.2 kilometers) through meadows flanked by wildflowers and teeming with bees and butterflies, including (as shown above) Virginia's state insect, the eastern tiger swallowtail (*Papilio glaucus*). Such meadows are magical places, as I share next in *Chapter Eleven*.

Nature continually astounds by her richness and diversity. Each of the nation's varied ecosystems has its unique character and beauty, whether the cacti-dominated, light-infused desert Southwest or the coastal rainforests of the Pacific Northwest with their majestic redwoods; the towering Rockies populated by elk, moose, and bighorn sheep or the semi-arid Sandhills atop Nebraska's massive Ogallala Aquifer; the pristine boundary waters of upper Minnesota or the swampy Everglades of south-central Florida; the lazy bayous of Louisiana or the Rhine-like Hudson River Valley; the craggy coasts of New England or any of hundreds of others that grace this biologically and geologically variegated country. But it's an ecological fact: Nowhere in the United States can one find such boundless natural variety as along the AT.

The AT's narrow corridor south of Ceres, Virginia, threads through several farm pastures where hikers often experience a big sky.

ELEVEN

Meadows

Ye who love the haunts of Nature,
Love the sunshine of the meadow,
Love the shadow of the forest,
Love the wind among the branches . . .
Listen to these wild traditions,
To this Song of Hiawatha.[1]

—HENRY WADSWORTH LONGFELLOW

BY-AND-LARGE, THE AT IS A FOREST TRAIL. Leave your sunscreen at home if you hike in summer. Direct sunlight seldom penetrates the dense hardwood canopy or ambient cloud to brightly light the forest floor. All is diffusely lit: soft edges, faint shadows.

Meadows, then, are rare treats. One breaks out of the enveloping gloom into unexpected brilliance. The contrast shocks the senses. Brooding yields instantly to euphoria. Views are long, perspectives wide. One sees where one has been and where one is headed. One grasps the lay of the land, the relation of mountains, valleys, fields, and sky. Having been lost in the trees, one finally sees the forest. Meadows widen our world-view: inner and outer. There are life lessons at the edge of a meadow.

Because meadows are rare, they top my list of the AT's many wonders. I'd be surprised if the aggregate length of meadow walks exceeds twenty miles out of the 557 miles of trail in the Virginias. Memorable meadows include Sky Meadows State Park; Cole Mountain and the ridge just to its north, bursting with blackberries; contiguous farm meadows south of VA 42 near Ceres, Virginia; and the incomparable upland meadows of Grayson Highlands. Here and there along the way are scattered teasers, the meadow-like pastures of isolated farms through which the AT has right-of-way.

By far the most wondrous of meadows in Virginia are the tundra-like upland balds of Grayson Highlands State Park and contiguous Mount Rogers National Recreation Area. These balds are not natural clearings; rather they're remnants from clear-cut logging operations during the late nineteenth century. Naively one would expect to encounter

Grayson Highlands State Park in southwestern Virginia has been dubbed "an alpine Eden" graced by "airy mountain meadows, gushing trout streams, rhododendron-filled forests, and a conglomeration of high peaks."[2] Truer words have not been spoken. (Also, see pages 61, top, and 62, bottom.)

utter devastation in a clear-cut area, but nature is resilient and has rebounded with a stark beauty that is altogether enchanting. After logging ceased, cattle grazed the highland meadows, keeping them "balded."

When Grayson Highlands became a state park in 1965, most cattle grazing ceased. What to do? Allow nature to reforest the meadows or keep them in their unnatural de-forested state? Counter-intuitively, the decision was made to preserve the balds. I, for one, am grateful. To keep the highlands free of invading brush, ponies replaced cattle as resident grazers (see page 154). The herd, now numbering 150, has adapted nicely to the highland environment, which can be harsh in the extreme. Semi-wild, the ponies have acclimated to humans but do not depend upon human intervention for food, care, or shelter.

Sadly, one meadow experience was a shock to this hiker. Who'd suspect that just north of a small clearing on Peters Mountain, with its long view into West Virginia, lies a massive construction site for the Mountain Valley Pipeline (MVP), a 303-mile interstate pipeline from natural gas fields in the Marcellus and Utica shale formations to a compressor station in Pittsylvania County, Virginia? As noted in the introduction, the MVP was

TOP: A meadow on Peters Mountain, a fifty-two mile (83.7-kilometer) ridge that straddles the West Virginia/Virginia border northwest of Roanoke, Virginia. Its elevation ranges from 2,300 feet (701 meters) to 4,073 feet (1,241 meters). Near here, the Mountain Valley Pipeline crosses the AT. **BOTTOM**: A few miles/kilometers to the south, the AT trail sign to Rice Field Shelter is hard to miss.

A fallen post, with its weathered trail blaze, once guided AT hikers through a pasture-meadow west of Sugar Grove, Virginia. The post will be replaced by volunteers during regular trail maintenance.

activated on June 14, 2024, despite relentless bipartisan resistance from unlikely coalitions opposed to the environmental and climatic impacts of the MVP. Pipeline developers must follow a "Restoration Plan," but, as in the case of mountaintop removal, no short-term measures can fully restore what nature took millions of years to create. The damage will last for generations, if not eons, even as great strides have been made nationwide and internationally in implementing ecological principles of design and planning into healing the land.[3]

TOP: Near Catawba, Virginia, the AT skirts the edge of a hayfield, with a mountain ridge in the distance.
BOTTOM: Not far from Slab Town Road near Sugar Grove, Virginia, NOBO hikers exit deep woods to share a pasture walk with nonplussed cows. Here, the Eastern white pine (*Pinus strobus*) offers a sense of what the AT will be like further north in the Mid-Atlantic states and in New England.

TOP: In mid-April, spring has barely touched this pasture-meadow traversed by the AT south of the historic Wilderness Road (Bland County Route 606).
BOTTOM: On the south side of VA 42 near New Castle, Virginia, the AT winds through tranquil pasture before entering a forest and then a designated wilderness.

Beyond this expansive meadow near Atkins, Virginia, a SOBO hiker will climb the distant mountains. Here, one can feel the "pull" of the Appalachians on the AT.

Geologists tell us that the Appalachians began to form 480 million years ago, during the Ordovician Period when most of Earth's landmass was collected into a single supercontinent called Gondwana. Formation of the mountains continued for another 200 million years. Experiencing the many geological features and sense of deep time in these mountains is ever-present when hiking the AT.

In contrast, meadows are typically new features to the landscape, most the result of human activities such as clear-cutting for timber or farmland, the recent husbandry of grazing animals, and the use of prescribed burns for management, a current practice borrowed from Indigenous peoples. Regardless of their creation and no matter the time of year, meadows are sacred spaces and ecological wonders, and time spent in an AT meadow is often magical, even life-changing.

In an essay entitled "The Meadow across the Creek," Thomas Berry (1914–2009), the well-known eco-theologian and cultural historian, reflected upon one of the most significant experiences of his ninety-five years on Earth:

The AT passes through a wetland meadow (top) adjacent to this scenic hillside farm near Interstate 81 at Groseclose, Virginia. The upland meadow (below) of Little Wilson Creek Wilderness is the summer home to a herd of wild ponies. Nearby, at the headwaters of Little Wilson Creek, is a high-elevation bog with many rare species of plants.

In early fall, this meadow along the AT just north of VA 42 near New Castle blazes with color.

> [I] was quite young . . . eleven years old. Down [the hill from our new house] was a small creek and there across the creek was a meadow. It was an early afternoon in May when I first wandered down the incline, crossed the creek, and looked out over the scene. The field was covered with white lilies rising above the thick grass. A magic moment, this experience gave to my life something that seems to explain my thinking at a more profound level than almost any other experience I can remember. It was not only the lilies. It was the singing of the crickets and the woodlands in the distance and the clouds in the clear sky.[4]

What Berry experienced is uncommon for human beings, tormented as we are by doubts, fears, and worries. Berry had witnessed a microcosm in perfect harmony, and that experience imbued a mental shift that lasted a lifetime: "The universe is a communion of subjects, not a collection of objects."[5] This was Berry's meadow epiphany, when at last he could find words for the ineffable.

Forest seclusion is conducive to reflection, contemplation, and focusing within. What I call "meadow openness" is a rarer treat, expansive and freeing. Both forest and meadow feed the soul, and each is to be cherished. On the AT, a wayfarer discovers the cornucopia of gifts to be found in both. Other kinds of magical moments are shared in the next chapter, *Chapter Twelve: Magic.*

Trail magic is often the gift of trail angels like Dave and Donna Seeley, who were dedicated summer caretakers of the Blackburn Trail Center near Round Hill, Virginia, when I visited there in 2019. Glowing comments on the FarOut trail app (formerly GutHook) attest to their generosity—and their lasagna.

TWELVE

Magic

The universe is full of magical things patiently waiting for our wits to grow sharper.[1]

—EDEN PHILLPOTTS

MAGIC IS A SECRET ELIXIR that keeps an AT hiker pushing on against fatigue, weather, and mishaps. The ATC identifies "trail magic" of three types:[2]

- Finding what you need most when you least expect it.
- Encountering unexpected acts of generosity that restore one's faith in humanity.
- Experiencing something rare, extraordinary, or inspiring in nature.

Trail magic can be as simple as water bottles stashed trailside on a blazing hot day or as uplifting as a brilliant sunrise atop Chestnut Knob.

Generally, the first two of the three types of magic on the AT often occur combined in the form of an unanticipated caloric treats provided free of charge at a trail crossing by a "trail angel": a hamburger grilled on the spot, a slice of pizza, a soda or beer, even ice cream. Calories are a hiker's fuel. According to Steve Sherman and Julia Older in their trail diary, *Appalachian Odyssey* (1977), young and fit male hikers simply cannot carry enough calories and invariably lose weight; women, on the other hand, tend to gain body mass and weight.[3] It must be a metabolic thing. If there is one thing I know from all the years I've hiked the AT it's this: Every distance hiker burns a prodigious quantity of calories, day after day after day. Surprise caloric treats that you haven't had to carry are magical indeed.

The second type of magic is often gifted by amateur and/or professional trail angels, both with hearts of gold. A hiker seldom encounters the amateur ones, for their random acts of kindness are just that: random and without fanfare. But thank goodness as well for professional trail angels, such as Dave and Donna Seeley, who manage hostels and trail centers; ferry hikers to-and-fro; cook high-calorie, low-cost breakfasts and dinners; and generally cater to the needs of hikers: physical and spiritual. In fact, in Virginia alone,

Trail magic can be found in tart apples from an old abandoned orchard near the Limberlost trailhead in Shenandoah National Park, Madison County, Virginia. Such remnant trees are memorials to a way of life that no longer exists in the park. More than 400 families were removed from their mountain homes when the park was created in 1936. Photograph by Scott Jost, from his magical book, *Shenandoah Valley Apples* (2013), and used by permission.

there are at now at least seventeen official Appalachian Trail Communities; that is, towns on or near the AT with volunteers at the ready to strap on their trail-angel wings.[4]

For the author, whose daily mileage is limited and caloric requirements are modest, the third kind of trail magic is most beguiling: other random, pleasant surprises—sensory, awe-inspiring, or historic. Here's an example: I recall at least two locations on Virginia's AT where the trail runs alongside or through apple orchards. These are often remnants from old farms, such as those abandoned after the creation of the Shenandoah National Park in 1936. Their apples are not the grocery store varieties. They're stunted, misshapen, and spotted, but they're free for the taking: Grab and go. And, after too much trail food, their natural tartness is wonderfully refreshing. Deer and bears love them, too.

Similarly, one never expects to find a granite memorial to a fallen war hero high on a ridge accessible only by foot or horseback. But there it is just off the AT: the Audie L.

A few feet from the AT on Brush Mountain near Catawba, Virginia, one finds the Audie L. Murphy Memorial commemorating Murphy's fatal plane crash in 1971. The marker, erected in 1974 by Veterans of Foreign Wars Post 5311 in Christiansburg, commemorates Murphy as the "most decorated veteran of World War II."

Murphy Memorial, on the ridgeline of Brush Mountain in Jefferson National Forest near Catawba.

Murphy, an icon of my parents' generation, was the most decorated American combat soldier of World War II. If that weren't enough fame for any one person, he was a movie star, too, mostly in Westerns, but also playing himself in the autobiographical war film, *To Hell and Back* (1955). And, for good measure, he was an accomplished songwriter.

Fame, though, is a Faustian bargain. Murphy, traumatized by his war experiences, suffered depression and addiction to sleeping pills. In 1971, just prior to his forty-sixth birthday, Murphy perished in a plane crash on Brush Mountain. Also killed were the pilot and four passengers. The memorial—decorated with flags, medals, and all manner of memorabilia—lies a few yards uphill from the crash site. It can be argued that every inch of the AT is sacred ground, but this spot is especially hallowed.

The AT crosses a livestock gate at a tree-hugger's delight: Keffer Oak, one of largest known white oak trees (*Quercus alba*) on the trail. In 2024, the last time it was measured, its height was eighty feet (24.4 meters), its crown was 116 feet (35.4 meters), and its circumference was 235 inches (597 centimeters). It is more than 300 years old.

Who erected this stone obelisk beside the AT? One hiker or many? And why? For me, the obelisk evokes a reverence for place, like a Japanese Zen garden incongruously located within a national park. Such unexpected finds are occasions to pause, reflect, admire, and wonder.

Neither does one expect to come upon the tree-hugger's delight, the Keffer Oak or a stone obelisk in the middle of nowhere or massive, ever-evolving rock cairns. The AT of the Virginias offers all kinds of magical moments and places from the extraordinary to the historic and the sublime, more than sufficient to keep this septuagenarian going. One of my ilk can't help but ponder how many more wonders a thru-hiker experiences.

ABOVE: This is one of several large rock cairns along a mountain ridge on the AT south of the Eastern Continental Divide, a significant portion of which forms the Virginia/West Virginia border along the Allegheny and Peters Mountains.

OPPOSITE TOP: A more than casual glance at this enormous natural rockfall of talus circumscribed by the AT at Blackrock Summit in Shenandoah National Park leaves a passing hiker bewildered. How is it possible that the edges of the fractured rock remain so sharp given the antiquity of the geologic volcanic events that produced the rockfall?

OPPOSITE BOTTOM: Trail magic includes any pleasant surprise, including a welcome outdoor shower heated by sunlight at the Blackburn Trail Center.

The AT holds historic surprises as well. One doesn't expect to find trailside a large plaque similar to those planted in national parks at points of historical interest. But there's one on the AT in Amherst County at Brown Mountain Creek, between U.S. 60 and the Lynchburg Reservoir. Here's an excerpt:

> As you travel north along the next 1.4-mile (2.3-kilometer) section of the Appalachian Trail, watch for the remains of an abandoned community. Freed slaves built and lived in this small farm community in the early 1900s. The memories and insights into life on Brown Mountain Creek came from a former resident, Mr. Taft Hughes, during an oral interview with the Forest Service.

Mr. Hughes's fond recollections, found online, bring to life details of Brown Mountain Creek's inhabitants, those formerly enslaved who thrived there for more than four decades. Following the Civil War, landowner and slaveholder Jesse Richardson freed thirty-nine enslaved African Americans. Most remained to become sharecroppers along this lowland creek. There they continued to live until 1920, when the U.S. Forest Service purchased the land. To the observant, relics of the community persist: a spring house and foundations of homes. It's difficult to know what credence to give to a vibe, but the ghosts of Brown Mountain Creek seemed relatively content when I passed through.

The AT crosses Interstate 81 twice: at Daleville near Roanoke and, much farther south, on a county road at Groseclose. Not too far from the latter crossing, in an old farmhouse on a country lane 200 yards off the trail, lies the Settlers Museum of Southwest Virginia. And nearby that, trailside, sits the one-room Lindamood Schoolhouse, established in 1894. I'd been forewarned of this magical spot by a NOBO, but he was cryptic about details, not wanting to mar my experience by giving too much away. And he was so right. Providing shelter from the sun and bugs, sustenance for body and soul and an oasis from digital overload, Lindamood Schoolhouse quickly became my kind of trail magic.

The building's exterior is weathered and unpainted yet is in decent repair. Backpacks lie on the front stoop, and a sign welcomes hikers. Inside, one steps into the late nineteenth century. The room appears almost exactly as it would have on the day the school closed in 1937 after four decades of continuous use: rows of two-seater desks, wood stove at center, portraits of presidents Washington and Lincoln, cursive writing on the blackboard. Oh, and a list of school rules and punishments for infractions on the wall opposite the blackboard. The only modern touches are three coolers along a wall: one filled with sodas, one with water, one with snacks. All for the taking, thanks to a local Methodist church with more than its share of trail angels.

There is, however, an altogether different form of magic on the AT that I'll call inner magic. It's exceedingly rare, but experiencing this kind of magic can last a lifetime.

TOP: Alongside the well-worn AT (lower right) near Groseclose, Virginia, sits the historic one-room Lindamood Schoolhouse where trail magic awaits.
BOTTOM: Note the portraits above the blackboard of Presidents Lincoln (top left) and Washington (top right) and how the American flag has but forty-four stars representing forty-four states. For a historic timeline, Wyoming became the forty-fourth state on July 10, 1890, four years before the school opened in 1894, and Utah became the forty-fifth state on January 4, 1896.

The front door of the Lindamood Schoolhouse, established in 1894, beckons hikers: Enter!

I've never been much of an athlete. Still, there have been rare instances when my actions in the moment seemed natural, effortless, and perfect. Here are a few examples:

In pee-wee football as a child, I once tackled our star athlete, hitting him so perfectly that he went down instantly but safely, neither of us the least bit hurt. I've played golf only a few times in my life, but I remember a magical stroke with an iron that connected so smoothly I felt no shock whatsoever, the ball traveling in a perfectly planar arc. During high school, I took flying lessons and soloed before I could drive. I learned to fly in a fabric-covered Aeronca Chief, an old tail-dragger, which entered full stall at touchdown. Once and only once, I landed so smoothly I never felt the wheels touch the runway. In high school, I also ran track, the half-mile and two-mile, but wasn't good enough to earn a letter. On one particular practice day, however, I ran what seemed to be a near-perfect half-mile, at least for me. Afterwards, the coach, who never gave me another compliment, said, "That's how you run the half-mile!"

Rising early on the AT has its rewards, such as this sunrise view of mountains and sculptural rock outcrops south of Daleville, Virginia, that resemble modern art.

I have also experienced magical moments on extended bicycle trips when I temporarily became one with the bike and the road, losing myself in the experience.

Such moments of inner magic are even rarer when backpacking, partly because it takes a critical mass of consecutive days on the trail before one drops into a groove. My section-hikes are usually limited to three or four days. But back in 1988, when I first hiked the high country of the Mount Rogers area, my fourth trail day was such a day: fifteen miles with a pack of at least forty pounds, without struggle, as if it were the most natural thing in the world.

There's an uncommon word for such moments: *plenitude*, the condition of feeling whole or complete. These rare openings upend one's views of self and of "normal" life. My "normal" life—isolated and insulated from nature, bombarded by noise and stimulus, compulsively busy—is unreal. *This*—walking the AT's forests and meadows—was what I, a bipedal hominid, was born to do. When walking the AT, I am ever in the moment: *this* moment.

It's sure to be a good day when a hiker awakens to a sunrise such as this over Burke's Garden, witnessed from 4,409-foot (1,344-meter) Chestnut Knob. (Also, see pages 99, 185, and 186.)

THIRTEEN

Postscript

For I have learned to look on nature,
not as in the hour of thoughtless youth;
but hearing oftentimes the still, sad music
of humanity.[1]

—WILLIAM WORDSWORTH

I'M PERCHED ON A GRASSY SLOPE atop Chestnut Knob. I'm in my tent, minus its rainfly, looking through my "porch" screen. To the north, the Knob commands the full sweep of Burke's Garden, a four-mile-by-eight-mile valley of oval shape, ringed by mountain ridges. Directly ahead is the Garden. To my left and right are thickets of wildflowers, buzzing with bees and fluttering with butterflies. The air at this elevation, even in August, is cool. It's approaching dusk, and, having rested for four hours after midday before making the long climb to the Knob, I am surprisingly relaxed, rested, and tranquil. There's no place I'd rather be at this moment.

Since I was a wee tyke, Tazewell County's Burke's Garden has enthralled me. Among my first memories are mesmerizing tales of the Burke's Garden Varmint. Luscious and verdant, the Garden was once ideal for raising sheep; that is, until something started killing the gentle creatures by ripping their throats and leaving the carcasses mostly intact. No local farmer could catch a glimpse of the elusive creature, let alone trap it. For a long while, the Varmint remained a mystery. That mystery infused and infected the imagination of a four-year-old. What might that varmint be? In desperation, Garden farmers hired an ace tracker from out West. Eventually, he trapped and dispatched the culprit: a lone coyote.

Adding to the aura of the Garden is its unusual geology. On a map or from the air, Burke's Garden looks like a volcanic caldera or, possibly even, a meteor crater. It's neither, geologists tell us. Rather, it's a gigantic sinkhole. All the water that gathers in the bowl runs toward the west, forms Wolf Creek, and cascades through a breach in the western rim.

A single paved road leads into the bowl, entering along Wolf Creek to circle the Garden's interior. In all directions, Garden Mountain rims Burke's Garden. Two dirt roads, five miles apart, cross Garden Mountain's imposing eastern ridge, the southern crossing at Walker Gap (elevation 3,500 feet). It's rugged country.

Then, too, my ancestry traces to the Garden. When Dad retired from his career in medicine, he bought a computer and took up genealogy as a hobby. When he neared the end of his life, he made us three kids swear on a stack of *Bibles* we'd not let his genealogical records be lost. On the issue of this promise, my conscience is not entirely clear. I found it easier to reconstruct Dad's research than to resurrect it from his archaic software. Still, this is the relevant part of what I found: *Both* of Dad's grandmothers—Roxie Lena Neal and Barbara Adeline Hager—were born in Burke's Garden.

Yesterday, I camped at the north end of the Garden, at the Davis Farm Campsite, 400 feet down the mountainside from the AT. It's the only other spot on Garden Mountain's eastern branch with a view, albeit circumscribed. Previous hikers had written on the sign at the short spur trail to the campsite: "Not worth it." I beg to differ, but for unique and situational reasons.

By intention, I left the Burke's Garden section to last, simply because I couldn't figure out how to manage it with my physical limitations. Southbound, there's a 1,600-foot climb; northbound, 2,000 feet. In between lies a ten-mile stretch with no reliable water sources. Given my limit of roughly eight miles per day, how was I to negotiate the climbs and distance without water?

Enter Davis Farm Campsite, the only location on the dry stretch with even a hint of water, "unreliable" according to both map and app, and a full half-mile off trail.

Damn the torpedoes. I entered Hunting Camp Creek Wilderness at 7:30 a.m., thanks to an early-morning shuttle by Bob Lingham, proprietor of Bear Garden Hiker Hostel. By 9:30, I'd knocked off more than four miles and arrived at the day's half-way point: Jenkins Shelter. After topping off water bottles, I began the slow, 1,600-foot ascent of Garden Mountain at around 10:00 and reached the spur trail to the campsite at 1:30 p.m.

All day long, I'd been anxious about the game plan and had devised Plans B and C, neither desirable. At the trail junction, the moment of reckoning had arrived. If there was no water at the campsite, I'd either bushwhack down Garden Mountain to the farms below or climb back to the ridge, hike another mile to VA 623, and then follow that dirt road for several miles into the Garden. Either plan had risks for a hiker parched and exhausted, and I was both.

Davis Farm Campsite is one of a kind. It's a postage-stamp-sized grassy rectangle barely big enough for two one-person tents. It's also the only level ground on a steep, nettle-strewn hillside. The one amenity is a narrow view of the Garden. The spot is level only because it was once the foundation of a tiny farmhouse belonging to the Davis family. Not

In the late afternoon, idyllic Burke's Garden in Tazewell County, Virginia, viewed from Chestnut Knob on Garden Mountain, presents as tranquil a scene as one is likely to behold on the AT.

lost on me: My paternal grandmother was Sheila Alice Davis. The family name of Davis is common in Burke's Garden, and Grandma's mother, Barbara Adeline Hager, who married William Drury Davis, was born there. Just possibly then, some of my ancestors had lived right where I'd camped. If so, they were a hardscrabble lot. To eke out a living in this rugged and isolated location would have required uncommon grit.

The one-tenth-mile path from the campsite to the iffy water source wound through waste-high stinging nettles that set my bare legs afire. Mercifully, there was water, but it was such a small flow there seemed no way to extract it. Close to panic, I recalled the trail engineering I'd seen previously and managed to anchor a broad leaf in the minuscule stream to construct a tiny spigot that trickled. It took ten minutes each to fill two water bottles. Three hours later, after dinner, I returned. The trickle had slowed to individual droplets. This time it took twenty minutes to collect only one-third of a liter. What a precarious edge we hikers of the AT sometimes tread.

Neither today nor yesterday did I encounter another soul on the trail. Just once during the last seven summers have I hiked in such complete solitude. Strange as it may sound, last night I took animal comfort from seeing the farms below, hearing the lowing of the cows at dusk and watching the moods of the Garden shift from afternoon to evening.

Having met the challenge of the arduous and risky first day, my spirits lifted as today progressed. I had just enough water to make Walker Gap, which promised two piped

From the Davis Farm Campsite on Garden Mountain, the moods of Burke's Garden follow the course of the day: (top to bottom) morning, early afternoon, late afternoon, and early evening.

springs on opposite sides of the dirt road. Earlier, at VA 623, trail angels had left five cans of Pepsi on a rock at the trail crossing (see page 196). I drank one, and in relief and gratitude, I nearly cried. God bless those angels!

Walker Gap afforded a temporary paradise. The northern of the two pipe springs flowed as promised in the guides. A 900-foot climb to Chestnut Knob awaited. No water there, so I set up base camp on the fire road by the spring. There, I replenished and treated water, napped, had an early dinner to avoid carrying water for dinner to the Knob, then napped again. The sun was bright, the air dry, the temperature perfect. Body and spirit recharged, I climbed to the Knob, arriving at 6:30 p.m.

Chestnut Knob Shelter is but one of few enclosed shelters on the AT of the Virginias. Originally the residence of the fire warden in the days of fire towers, the structure has been converted into a trail shelter. There's no fire tower now, but the concrete foundations remain. I opted not for enclosed shelter but to tent camp on the slope with the view.

It's a fitting end to my odyssey. What began unwittingly more than thirty years ago, when Dad dropped me in Damascus and I hiked north into the high country of Whitetop Mountain and Mount Rogers, continued in earnest six years ago, when Suzanne dropped me in Harpers Ferry and I set out to the south. More than two-dozen section-hikes between these bookends, and I have accomplished a goal that seemed ofttimes a pipe dream or folly: hiking the entire Appalachian Trail in the Virginias.

If all goes well tomorrow and the morning thereafter, I will return to Bear Garden Hiker Hostel. There, I will shower, visit briefly with hostelers Bob and Bertie, pick up my car, and drive home. If all goes as planned these next two days, I will have completed all of the AT in the two Virginias.[2]

I'm an anxious person, I confess. And solo hiking sometimes stokes that anxiety. There are so many ways to get into serious trouble. I don't usually relax until I'm back home. But at this moment in time, looking through my "porch" screen down onto Burke's Garden where my forebears—the Neals and Hagers and Davises—once lived, and some still do, hearing the bees buzz, and feeling a slight breeze in the ever-changing light, I am perfectly content. There is no place in this world I would rather be than where I am, high on the Appalachian Trail.

The author is ready to embark southbound (SOBO), near the Bear Garden Hostel, Ceres, Virginia. Photograph by Barbara Green, the author's sister, and used with permission.

GLOSSARY

Acronyms and Abbreviations

ACP Atlantic Coast Pipeline.

AT Appalachian Trail.

CCC Civilian Conservation Corps.

ATC Appalachian Trail Conservancy, headquartered in Harpers Ferry, West Virginia.

MVP Mountain Valley Pipeline.

NOBO An AT thru-hiker who travels northbound; that is, in the conventional southwest-to-northeast direction of the trail.

PATC Potomac Appalachian Trail Club, pronounced "Patsy," one of many volunteer organizations that maintain trails and trail shelters in the Virginias.

SOBO An AT thru-hiker who travels southbound; that is, against the traditional southwest-to-northeast direction of the trail.

SNP Shenandoah National Park.

Terms

bald A once-forested highland area that is now preserved in a meadow-like state.

blaze A mark on a tree, rock, or occasional post that indicates the AT (white) and its spur or side trails (blue). A double blaze signifies caution. Other colors (yellow, red, and orange) are used for trails not directly connected to the AT.

bubble A small group of AT thru-hikers that travel together for a brief time period.

bushwhack To traipse through the woods and underbrush without following a trail.

day-hiker A hiker who is enjoying the AT only for the day, without camping overnight.

Eastern Continental Divide The hydrologic divide in North America that separates the Atlantic Ocean watershed from the Gulf of Mexico watershed.

flip-flopper An AT thru-hiker who completes roughly half of the trail by walking either northbound and the remaining portion in the southbound direction or vice versa.

glamping Glamor camping; that is, camping with far more amenities than are essential.

hut See "shelter."

karst A subterranean topology laced with unstable caves and sinkholes formed when underground water dissolves soluble rocks such as limestone.

pasture-meadow A meadow that is also active pasture, usually where the AT crosses private farmland.

phenology The study of monitoring and recording annual and periodic changes in nature such as the times when a plant blooms, bird migrations, animals emerging from hibernation, and first and last frosts in autumn and spring.

ridgerunner A seasonal employee whose primary job is to educate and help AT thru-hikers.

section-hiker An AT hiker who is tackling the trail in sections that range in length from a few miles/kilometers to a few hundred miles/kilometers.

shelter Also known as a hut. Commonly a primitive, three-sided lean-to with a plank floor for sleeping and an exterior picnic table for communal meals, interspersed at semi-regular intervals along the AT. Rarely are AT shelters two-story or enclosed.

slack-packing Hiking a section of trail with a very light pack containing essentials only, while relying on nearby amenities for sustenance and lodging.

spur trail A side trail from the AT, marked with blue blazes by convention.

thru-hiker An AT hiker who attempts the entire trail in one continuous trek of several months duration.

trail angel Fellow human beings dedicated to the well-being of AT hikers by random acts of kindness or volunteer or professional services such as trail maintenance, hosteling, and providing snacks or meals.

trail magic A serendipitous and pleasant surprise while on the AT, such as finding a need satisfied when least expected, encountering an unexpected act of generosity, or experiencing a moment of indescribable beauty. Trail magic is often the result of the kindness of a trail angel.

trail name A unique pseudonym adopted by each AT thru-hiker, usually based on some defining personality trait or trail experience.

wilderness area A region of limited access to humans that is preserved in its wild or natural state. In the U.S., the Wilderness Act of 1964 both recognized the value to humans of wilderness and set aside the first of many such areas to be protected.

zero day A zero-mile "rest" day for long-distance hikers, usually devoted to gear- and self-maintenance.

NOTES

Acronyms

ACP	Atlantic Coast Pipeline
AT	Appalachian Trail
ATC	Appalachian Trail Conservancy
MVP	Mountain Valley Pipeline
VA	Virginia
WV	West Virginia

FOREWORD: 100 YEARS AND COUNTING

1. Benton MacKaye, as quoted in Jim Chase, *Backpacker Magazine's Guide to the Appalachian Trail* (Mechanicsburg, PA: Stackpole Books, 1989), xvi. Also, the two maps and captions that are presented on pages 8 and 12 appeared in Larry Anderson, *Benton MacKaye: Conservationist, Planner, and Creator of the Appalachian Trail* (Baltimore, MD: The Johns Hopkins University Press, in association with the Center for American Places, 2002), 149 and 187.

INTRODUCTION: HIKING THE AT

1. Charles Eisenstein is a popular speaker and writer whose books include *Sacred Economics: Money, Gift and Society in the Age of Transition* (Berkeley, CA: North Atlantic, 2011) and *Climate—A New Story* (Berkeley, CA: North Atlantic, 2018). The quotation comes from the essay, "Every Act a Ceremony," at his Website: https://charleseisenstein.org/essays/ceremony/.

2. The exact length of the Appalachian Trail (AT) is surprisingly hard to pin down, and different sources give different lengths. Upon reflection, it's easy to understand why. First, the AT is a living, breathing pathway that has evolved as conditions necessitate. Second, each hiker walks a unique AT, in the sense that no two hikers tread exactly the same footsteps. Over time, small differences in the paths of two hikers can accumulate to significant amounts. For the purposes of this book, however, we use as gospel the mileages posted by the Appalachian Trail Conservancy (ATC)—the official guardian of the trail—at the time of publication.

3. Trail mileages are taken from the "Explore" menu of the ATC's Website: https://appalachiantrail.org/explore/explore-by-state/.

4. Confession: I visited Dragons Tooth at the age of twenty while backpacking with two college buddies. Just prior to reaching this impressive rock formation from the south, the trail runs along a narrow groove in a massive slab of rock set at an angle of about seventy degrees to the horizontal. My fear of edges prevented my crossing this section while wearing a backpack, so I bypassed the section. As I recall, it felt challenging even in my youth, when the three of us traversed the section without packs and then used ropes to haul the packs up. In April 2023, at age seventy-four, I assuaged my conscience for having initially neglected six miles (9.7 kilometers) of the AT by conquering Dragons Tooth from the back side, on a day-hike with Pickle Branch Shelter as my base camp.

5. I hiked the twenty-four-mile section (38.6 kilometers) from VA 42 to the Mount Rogers National Recreation Area's Visitor Center in four days (May 6–9, 2019). Early on Saturday morning, May 11, my sister texted about an "incident" on the trail that closed the exact section I had just completed. Details trickled out over several days. The incident involved a knife attack on two hikers: one male, the other female. The female survived, though she was severely wounded; the male did not. The perpetrator was another hiker, trail name "Sovereign," well known to the AT community as mentally unstable and aggres-

sive. The victim, a forty-three-year-old wounded veteran known as "Stronghold," was universally beloved. The incident was widely reported, including in *The New York Times* (May 13, 2019): "Fatal Stabbing on the Appalachian Trail Is Uncovered Thanks to GPS and a Dog." Nature cannot completely insulate the AT community from the difficulties and demons that plague the larger society. Rest in peace, "Stronghold."

6. David Emblidge, editor, *The Appalachian Trail Reader* (New York, NY: Oxford University Press, 1996), back cover.

7. Details provided by Laurie Potteiger, Information Services Manager, ATC. For more information, see http://www.appalachiantrail.org/home/conservation. Of note, the Appalachian Trail Conservancy, The Conservation Fund, and the Roanoke Appalachian Trail Club worked as a coalition to purchase in December 2020 nearly 600 acres (243 hectares) on three private parcels of land in order to protect scenic vistas from McAfee Knob, which became even more popular after the release in 2015 of the movie, *A Walk in the Woods* (based on Bill Bryson's 1998 book). The purchase was aided by a large donation by the controversial Mountain Valley Pipeline (MVP) in Virginia (VA) and West Virginia (WV). As reported in "Virginia News Brief," *The Daily News Leader* (December 24, 2020): 5A.

8. Patrick Hite, "Cameras key to keeping trails clear: Couple has passion for maintaining area's natural resources," *The Daily News Record* (January 1, 2020): 1A and 2A.

9. Michael Martz, "Dominion cancels Atlantic Coast Pipeline, sells natural gas transmission business," *The Richmond Times Dispatch* (July 5, 2020); https://richmond.com/news/virginia/dominion-cancels-atlantic-coast-pipeline-sells-natural-gas-transmission-business/.

10. See, for example, Monique Calello, "On pipeline, 'I stood up to Dominion. And I won." and Robert "Bobby" Whitescarver, "It was more than just a pipeline we defeated," *The Daily News-Leader* (July 29, 2020): respectively, 1A–2A and 4B–5B; https://www.newsleader.com/story/news/2020/07/09/atlantic-coast-pipeline-i-stood-up-to-dominion-and-i-won-justice-for-schages-lane-augusta-county-va/5404821002/ and https://www.newsleader.com/story/opinion/2020/07/16/more-than-just-pipeline-we-defeated-atlantic-coast-pipeline-acp-staunton/5445175002/. Also, see Coral Davenport, "West Virginia Pipeline Is Halted Amid Conflict," *The New York Times* (July 13, 2023): A13; https://www.nytimes.com/2023/07/12/climate/mountain-valley-pipeline-courts.html; and Adam Liptak and Abbie Vansickle, "Supreme Court Clears Way for Pipeline Environmentalists Fought," *The New York Times* (July 28, 2023): A17; https://www.nytimes.com/2023/07/27/us/supreme-court-mountain-valley-pipeline.html; and Jonathan Mingle, *Gaslight: The Atlantic Coast Pipeline and the Fight for America's Future* (Washington, DC: Island Press, 2024).

11. Aldo Leopold (1887–1949)—the eminent wildlife biologist and ecologist who co-founded the Wilderness Society and established the idea of an American land ethic in his pioneering book, *A Sand County Almanac and Sketches Here and There* (Oxford, 1949)—believed in the importance of *phenology* as a fundamental ecological principle. He passed that belief on to his five famous scientist-children, including daughter Nina, who offered this summary of the word's meaning: "*Phenology* is the study of monitoring changes in nature; that is, recording annual and periodic natural occurrences, such as plant bloom times, bird migrations, and animals emerging from hibernation. The study of phenology especially considers the influence that weather, climate, and seasonal changes have on these events." As quoted in Nancy Nye Hunt, *Aldo Leopold's Shack: Nina's Story, a New Edition* (Staunton, VA: George F. Thompson Publishing, 2025), 90.

12. Benton MacKaye, as quoted in Jim Chase, *Backpacker Magazine's Guide to the Appalachian Trail* (Mechanicsburg, PA: Stackpole Books, 1989), xvi.

ONE: TRAILS

1. Benton MacKaye, "An Appalachian Trail: A Project in Regional Planning," *Journal of the American Institute of Architects*, Vol. 9 (October 1921): 325–30.

2. On July 28, 2015, REI's online journal, *Uncommon Path*, published an article by Zach Davis titled "21 Appalachian Trail Statistics That Will Surprise, Entertain and Inform You." Some are mundane. At least one (Fact #3) is astounding: "[O]ver the course of the Appalachian Trail's 2,189 miles, thru-hikers gain and lose over 464,464 ft., or more than 89 miles." [Note: The current length of the AT is 2,197.4 miles or 3,536 kilometers.] Do the math, and this is indeed the equivalent of sixteen 29,000-foot (8,839-meter) Mount Everests, from sea level to summit (https://www.rei.com/blog/hike/21-appalachian-trail-statistics-that-will-surprise-entertain-and-inform-you).

3. White blazes are used to mark the AT; blue blazes are used as markers for spur trails directly connected to the AT; other colors (yellow, red, and orange) are used for spur trails not directly connected to the AT.

4. On a day hike in April 2023, I completed the omitted section by hiking to Dragons Tooth from the south.

5. Indeed, at the time the AT was conceived in 1921, MacKaye was tending to a dark place in his own life: His wife had recently died by suicide. A friend, the architect Charles Harris Whittaker (1872–1938), invited MacKaye to a New Jersey farm to recover. There at the estate house, MacKaye shared his vision with Whittaker, and Whittaker, the editor of *Journal of the American Institute of Architects*, offered the journal as a forum for the vision. The fascinating story, "Where It All Began" by Anne Merrill, can be found in the Fall 2023 edition of *A. T. Journeys*: https://journeys.appalachiantrail.org/issue/fall-2023/.

6. MacKaye, op cit.

7. Ibid.

8. Ibid.

9. Ibid.

10. Ibid.

11. During the Cold War era, the site belonged to Bedford Air Force Station, one of many SAGE (Semi-Automatic Ground Environment) outposts of the early warning network. At that time, the facility housed three radar antennae, each protected from severe weather by a dome. In 1975, the U.S. Air Force decommissioned the installation and handed control to the Federal Aviation Administration (FAA), which continues to maintain a single radar antenna.

12. David Emblidge, *The Appalachian Trail Reader* (New York, NY: Oxford University Press, 1996), 72.

13. Ibid., excerpting from Guy and Laura Waterman, *Forest and Crag: A History of Hiking, Trail Blazing, and Adventure in the Northeast Mountains* (Boston, MA: Appalachian Mountain Club, 1989).

14. Henry David Thoreau, "Walking," *The Atlantic*, Vol. IX, No. 56 (June 1862): 657–74; as quoted on 665.

15. Johnson and Tierney.

16. Mills Kelly, *Virginia's Lost Appalachian Trail* (Charleston, SC: The History Press, 2023): 13, 29. In Kelly's riveting account of the re-routing of VA's AT, the issue of the Blue Ridge Parkway is what drove a permanent wedge between Benton MacKaye, the dreamer who envisioned the AT, and Myron Avery (1899–1952), the sometimes abrasive pragmatist who made it a reality. For MacKaye, who prioritized wilderness over completion, re-routing the AT was sacrilege. Following an angry exchange of letters, their relationship ruptured. The men never again spoke.

TWO: HIKERS

1. Aspen Matis, *Girl in the Woods: A Memoir* (New York, NY: HarperCollins, 2015).

2. Larry Bleiberg, "The Appalachian Trail for All," *AAA World* (August-October 2024): 36–38, especially 37.

3. Henry Wadsworth Longfellow, *Song of Hiawatha* (Boston, MA: Ticknor and Fields, 1855).

4. Lizzie Johnson and Lauren Tierney, "Why the Famed Appalachian Trail Keeps Getting Longer—and Harder," *The Washington Post* (July 27, 2023); https://www.washingtonpost.com/history/interactive/2023/appalachian-trail-length-route-changes/.

THREE: VISTAS

1. Rainer Maria Rilke. *Letters on Life: New Prose Translations*, edited and translated by Ulrich Baer (New York, NY: Modern Library, 2006).

2. Robert Frost, "Stopping by Woods on a Snowy Evening," in *The Poetry of Robert Frost*, edited by Edward Connery Lathem (New York, NY: Henry Holt and Company, 1923).

FOUR: WATER

1. Samuel Taylor Coleridge. "The Rime of the Ancient Mariner," in *Lyrical Ballads with Other Poems*, Vol. I (Second Edition) by Williams Wordsworth (London, UK: T. N. Longman and O. Rees, 1800).

FIVE: BRIDGES

1. Lyrics from Paul Simon's "Bridge Over Troubled Water," from Simon and Garfunkel's 1970 album by the same name. The song won five Grammys in 1971.

2. For a full history of the origins of "Shenandoah," see Warren R. Hofstra, "The Shenandoah Valley: Legendary American Landscape," in Andrei Kushnir, *Oh, Shenandoah: Paintings of the Historic Valley and River* (Staunton, VA: George F. Thompson Publishing, 2016), 17–38, especially 17–20.

3. Thomas Jefferson, *Notes on the State of Virginia* (Philadelphia, PA: Prichard and Hall, 1788), 18.

4. Ibid., 17.

5. William Shaffer, as quoted in Abigail Tucker, "The Army Veteran Who Became the First to Hike the Entire Appalachian Trail," *Smithsonian Magazine* (July 2017); https://www.smithsonianmag.com/smithsonian-institution/army-veteran-became-first-hike-entire-appalachian-trail-180963678/

SIX: WEATHER

1. Marcel Proust, *The Guermantes Way*, translated by Mark Treharne (London, UK: Penguin Classics, 2005).

SEVEN: SHELTERS

1. Lyrics from "Gimme Shelter," written by Mick Jagger and Keith Richards, the opening track of the Rolling Stone's 1969 album, *Let It Bleed* (1969).

2. William Shakespeare, *Macbeth*, Act 2, Scene 2.

3. Adapted from the Website of Woods Hole Hostel and Mountain B&B: http://woodsholehostel.com.

4. Victor Mather, "Slices of the Appalachian Trail Left Impassable in Many States," *The New York Times* (October 6, 2024): 15; https://www.nytimes.com/2024/10/05/us/appalachian-trail-helene-damage.html. Also, see, "Hurricane Helene Damage in Damascus Walking Tour," Friday's Forever, YouTube (October 28, 2024): 19:49 minutes.

EIGHT: SPURS

1. Robert Frost, "The Road Not Taken," in Edward Connery Lathem, ed., *The Poetry of Robert Frost: The Collected Poems, Complete and Unabridged* (New York, NY: Holt, Rinehart and Winston, 1969), 105; originally published in *Mountain Interval* (New York, NY: Henry Holt and Company, 1916).

NINE: FLORA

1. Robin Wall Kimmerer, *Braiding Sweetgrass: Indigenous Wisdom, Scientific Knowledge, and the Teaching of Plants* (Minneapolis, MN: Milkweed Editions, 2020), 298.

2. Chris Bolgiano, *Living in the Appalachian Forest: True Tales of Sustainable Forestry* (Mechanicsburg, PA: Stackpole Books, 2002), 5–6.

3. Adapted from "History of the American Chestnut" at the American Chestnut Foundation's Website: https://www.acf.org/the-american-chestnut/history-american-chestnut.

4. Henry Wadsworth Longfellow, "The Village Blacksmith," *The Knickerbocker*, Vol. 16, No. 5 (November 1840).

TEN: WILDLIFE

1. Chief Dan George, as quoted in G. W. Mullins, with original art by C. L. Hause, *Walking with Spirits: Native American Myths, Legends, and Folklore* (self-published, 2017).

2. Even as this is a myth, many have wondered if the U.S. would have been a less bellicose nation during its history had its national symbol not been a bird of prey.

3. See "About Pollinators," *The Pollinator Partnership*; https://www.pollinator.org/pollinators. Regarding the ongoing plight of butterflies, see Catrin Einhorn and Harry Stevens, "Study Documents 'Alarming' Butterfly Losses," *The New York Times* (April 1, 2025): D8.

ELEVEN: MEADOWS

1. Henry Wadsworth Longfellow, *Song of Hiawatha* (Boston, MA: Ticknor and Fields, 1855).

2. From the Blue Ridge Outdoors Website: https://www.blueridgeoutdoors.com/sponsored-content/insiders-guide-grayson-highlands-state-park-virginias-land-high-peaks-grassy-balds-wild-ponies/.

3. See, especially, two award-winning books: George F. Thompson and Frederick R. Steiner, editors, *Ecological Design and Planning* (New York, NY: John Wiley & Sons, 1997), and Frederick R. Steiner, George F. Thompson, and Armando Carbonell, editors, *Nature and Cities: The Ecological Imperative in Urban Design and Planning* (Cambridge, MA: The Lincoln Institute of Land Policy, 2016).

4. Thomas Berry, *The Great Work: Our Way to the Future* (New York, NY: Bell Tower, 1999), 12.

5. Thomas Berry, *Evening Thoughts: Reflecting on Earth as Sacred Community* (San Francisco, CA: Sierra Club, 2006), 149. The quotation is actually a popular paraphrase of Berry's actual statement: "The universe is composed of subjects to be communed with, not [a collection] of objects to be used."

TWELVE: MAGIC

1. Eden Phillpotts, *A Shadow Passes* (London, UK: Cecil Palmer & Hayward, 1918). The quotation, slightly modified, has also been widely but incorrectly attributed to William Butler Yeats or, occasionally, to Bertrand Russell.

2. From the Website of the Appalachian Trail Conservancy: https://appalachiantrail.org/explore/hike-the-a-t/thru-hiking/Trail-Magic/.

3. David Emblidge, *The Appalachian Trail Reader* (New York, NY: Oxford University Press, 1996), 75, quoting an excerpt of the trail diary of Steve Sherman and Julia Older, published as *Appalachian Odyssey* (Stephen Greene Press, 1977).

4. From southwest to northeast, VA's seventeen AT Communities are: Abingdon, Damascus, Marion/Smyth County, Bland County, Narrows, Pearisburg, Troutville, Glasgow, Buena Vista, Nelson County, Waynesboro, Harrisonburg, Elkton, Luray/Page County, Front Royal/Warren County, Berryville/Clarke County, and Round Hill; in WV, Harpers Ferry/Bolivar are jointly a trail community. Fifty-six communities along the entire AT corridor have been recognized by the ATC's "A.T. Community" program.

THIRTEEN: POSTSCRIPT

1. William Wordsworth. "Lines written above Tintern Abbey," in *Lyrical Ballads with Other Poems*, Vol. I, Second Edition (London, UK: T. N. Longman and O. Rees, 1800).

2. Of the 557 miles (896.4 kilometers) of the AT in Virginia, 25.3 miles (40.7 kilometers) of which are shared with West Virginia, I completed more than 500 (805 kilometers) in retirement, repeating several sections done years ago, among them Three Ridges, The Priest, Dragons Tooth, and Mountain Lake Wilderness. Full disclosure: I did not, however, repeat the section from Damascus to Mount Rogers, which I hiked in August 1988 at the age of forty. On September 11–12, 2023, as day-hikes, I claimed the last little section of VA's AT my feet had not yet trod: the 4.5 miles (7.2 kilometers) from the north end of Damascus to the Tennessee border. Twice in fact, given that both hikes, through town and to the state line, were up and back.

On the campus of old Storer College in Harpers Ferry, West Virginia, between the ATC's Visitor Center and the AT, stands this monument commemorating the awakening of "a guilty nation" to the injustice of slavery. John Brown's famous raid on Harpers Ferry (then in Virginia) on October 16–18, 1859, was an attempt to start an armed revolt by those enslaved to destroy slavery.

SUGGESTED READINGS

Articles

Gupta, Alisha Haridasani, "The Benefits of an Inclusive Outdoor Escape," *The New York Times* (July 19, 2022): D7; online at https://www.nytimes.com/2022/07/07/well/mind/ecotherapy-mental-health-diversity.html.

Harlan, Will, "Don't Cross the Appalachian Trail," *The New York Times* (February 24, 2020): A19; published online (February 23, 2020) as "Will the Appalachian Trail Stop an $8 Billion Pipeline? It's up to the U.S. Supreme Court."

Johnson, Lizzie, "For Appalachian Trail, a Pandemic of Popularity," *The Washington Post* (August 23, 2021): A1, 12, and 13; published online (August 22, 2021) as "Ruining the Roller Coaster: Can the Appalachian Trail survive its pandemic popularity?"

Johnson, Lizzie, and Lauren Tierney, "Why the Famed Appalachian Trail Keeps Getting Longer—and Harder," *The Washington Post* (July 27, 2023); https://www.washingtonpost.com/history/interactive/2023/appalachian-trail-length-route-changes/.

MacKaye, Benton, "An Appalachian Trail: A Project in Regional Planning," *Journal of the American Institute of Architects*, Vol. 9, No. 10 (October 1921): 325–30.

Marra, Sandra, "President's Letter: Shifting Perspectives and Realities," *A.T. Journeys* (Summer 2020): 8.

Books

Anderson, Larry, *Benton MacKaye: Conservationist, Planner, and Creator of the Appalachian Trail* (Baltimore, MD: The Johns Hopkins University Press, in association with the Center for American Places, 2008).

Berry, Thomas, *The Great Work: Our Way to the Future* (New York, NY: Bell Tower, 1999).

Bolgiano, Chris, *Living in the Appalachian Forest: True Tales of Sustainable Forestry* (Mechanicsburg, PA: Stackpole Books, 2002).

Brooks, Maurice, *The Appalachians* (Boston, MA: Houghton Mifflin Company, 1965).

Bryson, Bill, *A Walk in the Woods: Rediscovering America on the Appalachian Trail* (New York, NY: Broadway Books, 1998).

Chase, Jim, *Backpacker Magazine's Guide to the Appalachian Trail* (Mechanicsburg, PA: Stackpole Books, 1989).

Common Native Trees of Virginia: Identification Guide [no author] (Richmond: Virginia Department of Forestry, 2016).

D'Anieri, Philip, *The Appalachian Trail: A Biography* (Boston, MA: Houghton Mifflin Harcourt, 2021).

Eanes, Russ, *The Walk of a Lifetime: 500 Miles on the Camino de Santiago* (Harrisonburg, VA: Walker Press, 2019).

Emblidge, David, *The Appalachian Trail Reader* (New York, NY: Oxford University Press, 1996).

Fletcher, Colin, *The Complete Walker: The Joys and Techniques of Hiking and Backpacking* (New York, NY: Alfred A. Knopf, 1968).

Kaine, Tim, *Walk, Ride, Paddle: A Life Outside* (New York, NY: HarperCollins, 2024).

Kelly, Mills, *Virginia's Lost Appalachian Trail* (Charleston, SC: The History Press, 2013).

Kimmerer, Robin Wall, *Braiding Sweetgrass: Indigenous Wisdom, Scientific Knowledge, and the Teachings of Plants* (Minneapolis, MN: Milkweed Editions, 2013).

Letcher, Lucy, and Susan Letcher, *The Barefoot Sisters Southbound (Adventures on the Appalachian Trail)* (Mechanicsburg, PA: Stackpole Books, 2009).

Little, Charles E., *Greenways for America* (Baltimore, MD: The Johns Hopkins University Press, in association with the Center for American Places, 1990; paperback, 1995).

Little, Charles E., *The Dying of the Trees: The Pandemic in America's Trees* (New York, NY: The Viking Press, 1995; paperback 1997).

Mingle, Jonathan, *Gaslight: The Atlantic Coast Pipeline and the Fight for America's Future* (Washington, DC: Island Press, 2024).

Mittlefehldt, Sarah, *Tangled Roots: The Appalachian Trail and American Environmental Politics* (Seattle: University of Washington Press, 2014).

Montgomery, Ben, *Grandma Gatewood's Walk: The Inspiring Story of the Woman Who Saved the Appalachian Trail* (Chicago, IL: Chicago Review Press, 2014).

Moor, Robert, *On Trails: An Exploration* (New York, NY: Simon & Schuster, 2016).

Porter, Eliot, *Appalachian Wilderness: The Great Smoky Mountains*, with an essay on its natural and human history by Edward Abbey and an epilogue by Harry M. Caudill (New York, NY: Ballantine Books, 1973).

Ryan, Jeffrey H., *Blazing Ahead: Benton MacKaye, Myron Avery, and the Rivalry that Built the Appalachian Trail* (Boston, MA: Appalachian Mountain Club Books, 2017).

Strayed, Cheryl, *Wild: From Lost to Found on the Pacific Crest Trail* (New York, NY: Vintage Books, 2013).

Films

Beyond the Tree Line: Meeting the Four Year Old Conquering the Appalachian Trail, directed by Joel Guelzo (Freestyle Digital Media, 2024).

Into the Wild: My Journey on the Appalachian Trail by Julia Sheehan (YouTube, December 16, 2019).

Newsletters

A.T. Journeys: The Official Magazine of the Appalachian Trail Conservancy, published quarterly by the Appalachian Trail Conservancy, 799 Washington Street, Harpers Ferry, West Virginia 25425 (https://appalachiantrail.org/news-events/a-t-journeys-magazine/).
ATC Newsletters (https://appalachiantrail.org/news-events/newsletters/).

Podcasts

The Green Tunnel (https://www.r2studios.org/show/the-green-tunnel/): Hosted by AT historian Mills Kelly, this podcast "explores the history and culture of the United States' most iconic long-distance hiking trail."

Websites/Facebook Sites

Appalachian Trail Communities (https://appalachiantrail.com/appalachian-trail-communities/).

Harrisonburg Appalachian Trail Community (https://www.facebook.com/HarrisonburgATC/).

Konnarock Trail Crew (https://appalachiantrail.org/get-involved/volunteer/trail-crews/konnarock-trail-crew/).

Mount Rogers Appalachian Trail Club (MRATC: https://www.facebook.com/groups/482529228557719/).

Natural Bridge Appalachian Trail Club (NBATC: https://www.nbatc.org/).

Old Dominion Appalachian Trail Club (ODATC: https://olddominiontrailclub.wildapricot.org/).

Outdoor Club of Virginia Tech (OCVT: https://ocvt.club/).

Piedmont Appalachian Trail Hikers (PATH: https://path-at.org/).

Potomac Appalachian Trail Club (PATC: https://www.patc.net/).

Roanoke Appalachian Trail Club (RATC: https://www.ratc.org/).

Tidewater Appalachian Trail Club (TATC: https://www.tidewateratc.com/).

One of these Pepsis at a road crossing on Garden Mountain saved the author's bacon in August 2019.

ACKNOWLEDGMENTS

ACKNOWLEDGMENTS ARE SUPPOSED TO BE THOROUGH yet mercifully brief. I will breach the second tenet for two reasons. First, like all authors, I have many to thank. But it is uncommon to have benefactors in such a plethora of categories: biologists, hiking companions, trail angels, editorial angels, photographers, and financial backers among them. Second, as a septuagenarian, I feel a compulsion to reflect upon life, one enriched by jaunts in nature and companions along the way.

I first discovered the joys of hiking and camping as a Boy Scout during middle school and subsequently through an outdoor-oriented social club during high school. Most of what I know about the rugged outdoor life I learned from Russell Taylor, a fellow Scout and club member who passed away in 2022.

During high school and my early college years, memorable hikes were often in the company of two of my best friends: Sam Lambert and Jon Hall. On one such trek during winter break, Sam, Jon, and I hiked from my parents' back door on the western (West Virginia) flank of East River Mountain to Grandma's cabin on the eastern (Virginia) side. The next morning, we awakened to ten inches (25.4 centimeters) of virgin snow. The beauty and intense quiet of our long slog home through the snow-covered wilderness, with Jon wearing sneakers, remain vivid.

I was with Sam when I took my first bona fide backpacking trip, also on East River Mountain. My earliest AT backpacking buddy was my brother, Willie. Thanks, Will, for being such a good sport on those early, challenging escapades. And a tip of the hat to my old friend, Ned Stephenson, for companionship during numerous outdoor adventures and misadventures over the course of a fifty-three-year friendship. These include bookend treks on both sides of the Tye River watershed: a frigid winter backpacking trip in 1972 on Three Ridges Mountain and a sweltering day-hike in July 2021 to the summit of The Priest.

During my early graduate school days, Bob Evatt and I survived several backpacking trips in winter, including one to the Grand Canyon in Arizona in March 1983. On the morning of our ascent from the Colorado River, we departed Phantom Ranch in fifty-five degrees Fahrenheit (12.8 Celsius) and misty rain. Six hours later and a mile (1.6 kilometers) higher, we crested the South Rim in eight inches (20.3 centimeters) of snow.

A special thanks to my younger friend, Tuan Nguyen, for accompanying me into the high country of Mount Rogers National Recreation Area when I was in my early forties and for encouraging me to keep backpacking, age be damned. In later life, I've cherished the annual outdoor adventures (including three backpacking trips) of the Compadres of the Campfire, now all in their seventies or eighties, about whom you'll hear more: Virgil Johnson, Wendell Fuqua, Bob Bersson, George Hillow, Scott Milliman, and Bob Detrich.

"I got a lifetime of camping in the Army" was Dad's motto after spending the winter of 1944–1945 in a foxhole in France. So Dad was neither a hiker nor a camper, but he was my original trail angel, happy to provide logistical support for his sons. On at least three occasions, Dad drove Willie and me to a trailhead near home and picked us up a few days later. And the week of his retirement in August 1988 he set me on the AT in Damascus and met me five days later near Sugar Grove. Thanks, too, Mom, for encouraging my summer stints as a camp counselor at Peaks of Otter Royal Ambassador Camp, where I first found a home and contentment in the Appalachian forest. Miss you, Mom and Dad.

Nowadays, trail angel *numero uno* is Suzanne Fiederlein, my wife. Suz has selflessly provided both logistical and moral support for my wanderings. On numerous occasions, she either ferried me to a trailhead hours from home or picked me up at the end of a hike. Thrice she's rescued me from mishaps minor and major, including a torn meniscus. Although not given to backpacking, she loves day-hiking. Together, we've trekked the Cinque Terre in Italy, trails in southern Arizona and Glacier National Park in Montana, and lovely sections of the AT in the Virginias, including the Henry Lanum Loop Trail, Crabtree Falls, and several blue- and red-blazed trails in Grayson Highlands State Park.

Our daughter, Elena ("Ellie"), has been hiking with her parents since she was three and is now an avid hiker, international backpacker, and rock-climber. She also ferried me into Shenandoah National Park for a section-hike once when Suz was away. Thanks, "Kiddo."

Virginia's Shenandoah Valley offers a cornucopia of nearby trails. For three decades and counting, much of our family's social life has revolved around hiking those trails with friends too numerous to list fully. Among these many are Bob Bersson, Jon Monroe and Andrea Pesce and family, Peter and Linda Kohn, Chris and Gene Bowlen and family, and Roshna Wunderlich.

Another shoutout goes to my sister and brother-in-law, Barbara and Wayne Green. The Green "Airbnb" provided a launching pad for two AT section-hikes near Bluefield, West Virginia. Both times they ferried me to the starting gate. The photo of the author on page 188 is by my sis. Speaking of kin, Justin Hawkins, aka "Sunrise Chaser," thru-hiked the AT in 2016 and belongs to my extended family. Thanks, Justin, for the two photographs of the ponies in Grayson Highlands on page 154.

A perk of living long is accumulating friends from many walks of life in many places. Charlie and Penny Finn ferried me to my car after an injury-prone section-hike that ended in Daleville. Marilyn Lerch, a college friend, graciously dropped me at U.S. 311 for a section-hike near Dragons Tooth. (Serendipitously, as this book's editorial development was nearing completion, Marilyn gave me Mills Kelly's fascinating account of 2023, *Virginia's Lost Appalachian Trail.*) Speaking of college days and Dragons Tooth, over spring break in

1969 Ralph Stinson, Bill Huber, and I hiked an AT section that included Dragons Tooth, spending our second night in a corn crib.

I also have Bob Bersson—fellow Compadre, band leader, writer, and biking companion—to thank for many of my current life's best moments. In 2015, Bob met me at U.S. 522 near Front Royal after my section-hike of Sky Meadows State Park. Later that summer, Bob, his brother-in-law, Phil Shoup, and I hiked a section of Shenandoah National Park, most of it in the rain, narrowly avoiding a rogue bear. In 2016, he, Bob Detrich, and I day-hiked the thirteen miles (20.9 kilometers) from Reeds Gap to the Tye River. And for my northernmost section-hike of Shenandoah National Park back in 2014, Bob and Wendell Fuqua ferried me to the trailhead and walked with me the first few miles/kilometers. The previous year, Wendell, Scott Milliman, and I did a short overnight to Rhododendron Gap on the AT from Grayson Highlands State Park, and in 2017 this trio also backpacked the Henry Lanum Loop Trail.

My original attempt of Garden Mountain was with Tom Crockett and several of his long-term hiking friends. Sick with a cold, I had to bail after one night of hacking at Jenkins Shelter. And thanks to Ray Ewing for hiking a few miles/kilometers with me during my early days on Northern Virginia's AT, where Ray introduced me to the Blackburn Trail Center.

For several section-hikes, I've relied on professional trail angels to ferry me to the starting point or return me to my car once the section was completed. These include Homer Witcher of Daleville, Don Raines and Tom Hoffman of Pearisburg, and Bob Lingham of Ceres. The photo of me at the Dismal Creek suspension bridge on page 83 is by Don. I don't know the name of the trail angel who placed five cans of Pepsi Cola on a trail-side rock on nearly waterless Garden Mountain in 2019 (page 200), but, whoever you are, your kindness was a life-saver.

With regard to editorial angels, few rank with Eileen Dight. Eileen's a Brit now living in Ireland, but distance does not diminish friendship. For more than a decade, Eileen has provided me unwavering support for all matters literary.

My wife, Suzanne, also belongs in this camp. She's got a sharp eye for errors and caught numerous typos that escaped others' attention. Old high-school friend Paul Coleman has an equally sharp eye for visual images. Thanks, Paul, for alerting me to photographs that weren't up to snuff.

Thanks to Karen Atwood for a random act of kindness forty years ago: the gift of Eliot Porter's photographic essay, *Appalachian Wilderness* (1973). When scratching my head for a model book format, I recalled Porter's luminous book and found it on a bookshelf at home. Karen's also a photographer and birder. Her photos of a deer (page 148) and a scarlet tanager (page 152) are included herein. And a special shoutout to Karen's *consuegra*, Cindy Robinson, for her two amazing photos of American black bears on page 151.

Sections herein of the *Introduction* and *Chapter Two: Hikers* were adapted from the anthology of Bob Bersson and Jack Greer: *Better with Age: Creativity, Discovery & Surprise* (Cove River Press, 2020), essays about aging to which I contributed "Hiawatha: Never Too Late for a Trail Name" (a variant of which also occurred in the online journal, *Like the Dew*, August 13, 2018). Jack, the percussionist in our band, a former seafaring sailboat owner, and a writer's writer, is the author of *Abraham's Bay & Other Stories* (Dryad Press, 2009). Thanks, Jack, for your surgical editorial skills and friendship.

To plant biologists Jonathan Monroe, Conley McMullen, and Oliver Hyman at James Madison University: Thank you for yeoman's work in identifying plant species from photographs. Your task was not easy, given the lack of physical specimens, and the author bears responsibility for any misidentifications.

To publisher George F. Thompson, I owe so much. George and I go back a ways as members of a monthly breakfast group, and it is a great fortune to count a publisher also as a friend. I know of no other who captures the essence and importance of place—"urban, rural, social, and wild"—better than George. His aesthetic eye is almost infallible, and his dedication to storytelling and publication excellence is unmatched. George invested considerable time and energy in sequencing the photographs, editing the text, and developing this project before either of us was certain it would come to fruition. His encouragement helped turn a pipe dream into reality. It's also been a joy to work with Mikki Soroczak, George's editorial and research assistant, who took a draft manuscript built with archaic software and transformed it into a work of art. And thank you, David Skolkin, for your artful book design.

Finally, I thank Mills Kelly, Appalachian Trail historian and host of the podcast, *The Green Tunnel*, for his gracious foreword, and the Appalachian Trail Conservancy and their all-volunteer trail clubs, for tireless stewardship of the AT. What a labor of love. And I extend special thanks to the many kindred spirits among the Harrisonburg Appalachian Trail Community, for their generous financial support, as well as the following individuals: Martha Merz, Bob Bersson, Eddie Bumbaugh and Jane Cox, Wendell Fuqua, Rich Gibson, Doug Hendren (with whom I take the weekly "Doug walk") and Nancy Beall, Andy and Bonnie Higgins, Scott Milliman, and Dick and Lois Wettstone. Rich, by the way, completed the AT in 2009 in two long section-hikes. And Eddie, Andy, and Dick, following two decades of section-hiking, planted their victory flag (figuratively) on Maine's Mount Katahdin in 2020, all pushing seventy.

INDEX

Note: Illustrations and caption references appear in *italics*.

ABOUT THE ESSAYIST

Mills Kelly was born in 1959 in Roanoke, Virginia, and grew up in Falls Church, Virginia. He received his B.A. in history at the University of Virginia and his M.A. and Ph.D. in history from George Washington University. He joined the faculty of George Mason University in 2001, where he was Professor of History and a Senior Scholar at the award-winning Roy Rosenzweig Center for History and New Media until his retirement in 2024. He has been hiking the AT since 1971, is the archivist for the Potomac Appalachian Trail Club, and is the maintainer of the Manassas Gap Shelter, one of the original shelters built along the AT during the 1930s. Professor Kelly has received numerous grants and fellowships from the Andrew W. Mellon Foundation, National Endowment for the Humanities, Virginia Foundation for the Humanities, and U.S. Department of Education. His books include *Virginia's Lost Appalachian Trail* (The History Press, 2023), *Teaching History in the Digital Age* (University of Michigan Press, 2013; 2016), and *Without Remorse: Czech National Socialism in Late Habsburg Austria* (East European Monographs/Columbia University Press, 2007), and a forthcoming history of the Appalachian Trail as told from the perspective of hikers. Professor Kelly also hosts a podcast, *The Green Tunnel*, "which explores the history and culture of the United States' most iconic hiking trail, the Appalachian Trail."

ABOUT THE AUTHOR

Dave Pruett was born in Durham, North Carolina, in 1948 and grew up in Bluefield, West Virginia. He received his B.S. in mechanical engineering from Virginia Tech and his M.S. and Ph.D. degrees in applied mathematics from the Universities of Virginia and Arizona, respectively, which enabled a career as a computational scientist and academic applied mathematician. That career includes a decade of experience in the aerospace industry at NASA Langley Research Center and three decades in the classroom, teaching mathematics and computational science in Virginia at J. R. Tucker High School in Henrico County and at four universities: Virginia Commonwealth University, the College of William and Mary, James Madison University (JMU), and Eastern Mennonite University. While a full-time faculty member in the Department of Mathematics and Statistics at JMU, Dave garnered a number of teaching awards, including the first Mengebier Endowed Professorship and the first Provost's Award for Excellence in Honors Teaching, the latter for a groundbreaking honors course that explored the interface between science and spirituality. In 2012, *Reason and Wonder*, his love letter to the cosmos and a spinoff of honors teaching, was published by Praeger. The American Library Association honored *Reason and Wonder* with a Choice Award shortly following its publication.

For more than half his life—including time growing up in Bluefield and thirty years residing in the Shenandoah Valley—Professor Pruett has lived in the shadow of the Appalachian Trail. All those years it beckoned, but it wasn't until 2013 when Pruett, semi-retired, could fully heed the call. In 2023, eleven summers of section-hikes later, Pruett, at age seventy-five, completed the entire AT through Virginia and West Virginia. He lives in Harrisonburg, Virginia—thirty minutes from the Skyline Drive and the AT. When he isn't hiking, he is most likely making music with the Countryside Garage Band or biking on the many rails-to-trails pathways he has recently discovered. Pruett is married to Suzanne Fiederlein, Executive Director of JMU's Center for International Stabilization and Recovery from 2020 until her retirement in 2025, and an eager hiking and biking companion. They have one daughter, Elena, a millennial and avid hiker, rock climber, and backpacker.

ABOUT THE BOOK

Hiking the AT in the Virginias: A Septuagenarian's Journey was published in an edition of 1,500 softcover copies with gatefold flaps. The text was set in Garamond and Din, the paper is Gardamatte Art, 80-pound weight, and the book was professionally printed and bound by Friesens in Canada.

Project Director: George F. Thompson
Editorial and Research Assistant: Mikki Soroczak
Manuscript Editor: Purna Makaram
Book Design and Production: David Skolkin

Special Acknowledgment: The publisher extends grateful thanks to the Diane Elizabeth Thompson Workman Fund of the Center for the Study of Place for making it possible to publish this book.

Published in 2025. First softcover edition.
Printed in 2025 on acid-free paper.

34 33 32 31 30 29 28 27 26 25   1 2 3 4 5

The Library of Congress Preassigned Control Number is 2025936092.

ISBN: 978-1-960521-07-1